Easy Small Business Ideas

How To Get Motivated, Multiply Your Customers, & Starve Your Competition

Fraser Druet

ISBN: 978-1-9995771-7-9

"This is a book filled with the foundational information that will help clarify, transform, and grow your business to become a top performer in your market."

— **Shep Hyken, bestselling author of** *I'll Be Back: How to Get Customers to Come Back Again and Again* **(www.IllBeBackBook.com)**

"Going through the exercises in Easy Small Business Ideas gave me clarity and a plan for maxing out the real estate clients I can help in my area. I found it insightful and easy to follow too."

— **Craig Walker, Platinum Club Realtor, RE/MAX**

"Get the motivation to start and the desire to keep going! Packed with simple, easy to learn, and easy to do business ideas, "Easy Small Business Ideas" will not only give you tons of inspiration to kick start your business but will also show the pitfalls and show you how to succeed. A must-read for young entrepreneurs, highly recommended!"

— **Reviewed by Laura, TheBigReads**

1. WRITE DOWN 5 PEOPLE YOU SPEND THE MOST TIME WITH, OUTSIDE OF FAMILY. WRITE DOWN 5 NEAREST TOP5 PEOPLE YOU KNOW OF.	2. WRITE DOWN NEGATIVE PARTS OF YOUR COMFORT ZONE. WRITE DOWN NEW POSITIVE CHANGES TO YOUR COMFORT ZONE YOU WANT.	3. WRITE DOWN LIST OF THINGS YOU NEED RIGHT NOW, THINGS WANT AT SOME POINT, AND PERSONALITY QUALITIES YOU NEED TO GUARANTEE SUCCESS.	4. CREATE YOUR 30-DAY VISUALIZATION SCHEDULE SHEET.
5. PUT A STICKY-NOTE REMINDER ON BATHROOM MIRROR TITLED "MAKE MY BED."	6. CALL LEADS WITHIN 1-MINUTE. MAKE AT LEAST 6 CALL ATTEMPTS FOR EVERY UNREACHED LEAD. IDEALLY BETWEEN 8-9AM AND 4-6PM.	7. SETUP AND USE A CRM CONSISTENTLY (IF COMMON ENOUGH IN YOUR INDUSTRY).	8. ALWAYS FOCUS EVERY SECOND OF THE CALL ON GETTING QUALIFIED PROSPECTS CLOSER TO CONVERTING.
9. FIGURE OUT WHAT UNIQUE ASPECT OF YOUR BUSINESS IS BETTER THAN WHAT ALL YOUR LOCAL COMPETITION CAN OFFER.	10. COMPLETE THE TIME MANAGEMENT CIRCLE EXERCISE.	11. SIGN UP FOR A LEAD-GENERATION SERVICE TO GET A STREAM OF CUSTOMERS TODAY.	12. SIGN UP FOR AN SEO SERVICE TO GET A STREAM OF CUSTOMERS IN THE FUTURE.
13. SIGN UP FOR REPUTATION MANAGEMENT TO MAXIMIZE YOUR POSITIVE REVIEWS.	14. HIRE A SOCIAL MEDIA MANAGEMENT SERVICE TO PROVIDE VALUABLE CONTENT TO YOUR PROSPECTS AND SHOW YOU'RE AN ACTIVE BUSINESS.	15. CALCULATE YOUR LTV. USE THIS CALCULATION TO FIGURE OUT HOW MUCH YOU CAN SPEND ON EACH AD VECTOR TO GET A CUSTOMER. AND ALSO USE IT TO KNOW HOW MUCH YOU CAN SPEND TO GET A REFERRAL.	16. MAKE A DREAM 100 LIST OF YOUR BEST POTENTIAL CUSTOMERS. SEND LIST MEMBERS LUMPY MAIL AND FOLLOW-UP CALLS EVERY 2 TO 4 WEEKS.

Get more ideas at FraserDruet.com

READ THIS FIRST

As a way of saying thank you for buying my book, here is a link to my 1-page printable '**Exercise Reminder Chart**' 100% FREE!

It will make the end-of-chapter exercises easier to track and complete. It includes a summary of the exercises for each chapter. You can print it out and cross off the exercises as you complete them and grow your business.

TO DOWNLOAD GO TO:

https://FraserDruet.com/BookBonus

Dedicated to the top 5%. Those who actually finish what they set out to accomplish. Those who take massive action. Those who do whatever it takes.

"A lobster, when left high and dry among the rock, does not have the sense enough to work his way back to the sea, but waits for the sea to come to him. If it does not come, he remains where he is and dies, although the slightest effort would enable him to reach the waves, which are perhaps within a yard of him. The world is full of human lobsters; people stranded on the rocks of indecision and procrastination, who, instead of putting forth their own energies, are waiting for some grand billow of good fortune to set them afloat."

— Dr. Orison Swett Marden

TABLE OF CONTENTS

CHAPTER ONE

Introduction

My name is Fraser Druet, and I'm going to show you how to get motivated into results, multiply your customers without spending a cent more, and leapfrog your competition with cutting-edge tools and strategies.

Throughout my university career and beyond, I'd approached life as a problem to be solved. I looked for insight within courses on tape from esteemed university professors. I devoured every history, finance, and philosophy course I could find.

I spent every spare moment listening to them. I later tallied it all up and found I'd completed two undergraduate degrees worth of courses.

I saw life as the "Gordian knot" problem Alexander The Great faced. This was a complex knot puzzle tied by a Greek king. Whoever undid the knot was destined to rule all Asia. Alexander solved it by slicing through it with his sword.

And I saw life as that knot. Full of many problems, ideas, riches, and unknowns. I was searching for a sword to slice through it all, as Alexander did. Throughout my studies, I felt close, but never quite found an answer.

I started drifting through life disillusioned and barely making ends meet. I went through a phase of trying all sorts of jobs. I was a data analyst, assembly-line worker, electrician, snow-shoveler, roughneck, programmer, and more.

Nothing felt right.

Then one day years later, I lucked out and discovered copywriting. It's the science of writing more persuasively. I'd finally found my sword.

I was in love.

I went out and bought every major book, course, and seminar I could get my hands on. I mean everything. Just as I had gone all out with my prior studies.

I spent more than 3100 hours pouring through the various lessons on copywriting, motivation, phone sales, Facebook ads, Google ads, sales funnels, marketing studies, different business niches, email marketing, business management, sales in general, and beyond.

This included over 108 books, seminars, and courses. Some courses had over 200 hours of material each.

I wrote over 2319 pages of notes. I filled five big Tupperware containers full of index cards I'd written special notes and ideas on. Thousands of cards worth.

I listened while driving, walking to the gym, eating meals, brushing my teeth, cooking, buying groceries, in the shower, folding laundry, playing video games, walking on the beach, and beyond. I dedicated every spare second of my day to learning more.

I was driven. I went on a learning frenzy with the same passion a Great White goes on a feeding frenzy. I studied it throughout the day and...

I Dreamt About

It At Night!

Some material I even consumed multiple times. I didn't just want to learn these successful ideas, I wanted to BECOME them.

I had dreams of replicating very lucrative and exciting marketing experiments.

I'd invested every cent I had into my marketing education... along with every cent I didn't have too.

I was in debt. I'd gained 45 lbs (I was fond of 13,000 calorie "Elvis sandwiches"). My health was fading away from stress.

Fig. 1. One of my 13,000 calorie "Elvis sandwiches." Recipe Credit: Elvis Presley

I realized it would take a lot of capital to do the kind of profitable marketing experiments I wanted. To slice through the Gordian knot of life, I'd need a source of consistent income.

I needed a way out of this hole. I needed a way to generate the capital required to test money-making ideas I'd collected over my studies.

Then I finally found the answer.

I could focus my marketing expertise on helping small businesses across North America and beyond. I figured the more value I generated them, the more value I'd get in return. Most considered extra patients, clients, and customers to be very valuable. This even helps influencers who want to grow their social media following online.

I started applying my expertise to small businesses. My marketing education had finally paid off. I was getting clients better results than most of the marketing bozos they'd tried before me.

Since then, I've generated customers for a wide variety of business niches. Niches such as:

- Dentists
- Roofing Companies
- Realtors
- Attorneys
- Chiropractors
- Wedding Photographers
- Insurance Salespeople
- Podiatrists
- Towing Companies
- HVAC Contractors
- Electrical Contractors
- Plumbers
- Yoga Studios
- Hair Salons
- Gyms
- MediSpas & Wellness Centers
- Cosmetic Surgeons
- Restaurants
- Financial Planners

And so on.

Basically if any business needed more customers, I found a way to make them happy with lessons learned from similar industries.

With each new happy client under my belt, my stress lowered, and so did my debt load. My health returned, and my weight bounced back to prior levels too.

As I worked with more and more niches, I learned more and more ways to make their businesses more profitable. I found an idea that made it easier for a roofing client to take calls also helped similar realtor clients. And I saw an idea that worked well for a chiropractor to keep track of leads also helped mortgage brokers. And so on.

I even started noticing success patterns both in current clients and prospective clients. These patterns were similar in the top 5% of performers across different industries. And these patterns didn't involve being born rich. They didn't involve being a supermodel, having a super-genius IQ, or anything like that.

They were simple daily attitudes and actions anyone could do. With them, they could propel themselves to the top 5% in their field and multiply their income. I started encouraging my other clients to adopt these practices. They were shocked at how simple, yet impactful they were.

Now I'm going to use this book to give you the same success ideas, strategies, and actions of top 5% performers. The ones they use to get maximum results in their business.

In fact, the main reason why I wrote this book was to specifically help my own clients succeed as quickly, easily, and greatly as possible. This way they would have both the motivation and the surplus profits to happily do business with me (and send me referrals) over the years to come.

That's also one of the reasons why I'm not holding anything back.

I want to give you everything possible to help identify and eliminate any profit bottlenecks. And I want to give you these solutions as efficiently as possible without making a book that's several thousand pages long.

Note: I will generally be referring to clients and patients as 'customers' throughout this book to simplify things.

So who is this book for?

This book is for people who want to get motivated, multiply their customers, and leapfrog their competition.

This involves changing your mindset to that of a top 5% performer and then taking massive action. You'll gain cutting-edge motivational strategies. These will help outline your life and business vision and get yourself on the optimal success path. Then you'll apply certain best practices to your current business to multiply your results (most of these won't cost a cent more). You'll also take advantage of numerous online (and offline) opportunities. I'll show you how they can help grow your business and leapfrog your competition.

The chapters in the motivation section may recommend drastic and hardcore ideas to promote positive change. These ideas will take many outside their comfort zone. But I promise they are no more hardcore than the ideas recommended by popular success coaches. Plus I paired them with other ideas in a powerful new combination.

This book isn't for someone who expects money to fall out of the sky because they own this book. (Likely unopened on their bookshelf). Most people are like this. The vast majority of people don't do anything to further their goals. Only the top 5% performers and beyond desire success enough to take action to achieve it.

Massive action = massive results. And the readers who finish the book and take massive action will get maximum results.

On the other hand, I want you to understand something important. If you aren't where you want to be in business or in life, then it's not your fault. You just haven't run across a teacher or friend or peer to show you a better way. A way that will fill in any missing pieces and jumpstart your journey toward where you really want to be. You only need to take action.

One quick tip before we start. I learned a way you can help keep yourself focused and increase reading speed, comprehension, and retention. You can do this all by reading the digital or physical book as you listen to the audiobook. Studies have been done showing that not only can you maximize your knowledge and comprehension by learning something more times. (Up to 17 times in fact). But it also further helps to learn it in multiple formats. So not just reading, but audio, video, in-person, teaching it to others (and even writing books on it).

So you'll be getting a kinda 2-for-1 knowledge deal this way. I've priced my audiobook and ebook as low as the platforms will allow, so this isn't a scheme to make an extra buck. It felt like mentioning this in the first chapter would help maximize what you get out of this book.

Now, let's get started.

PART ONE

GET MOTIVATED INTO RESULTS

CHAPTER TWO

The Secret To Becoming A Top Performer

What is the secret to becoming a top performer?

Is it a matter of money?

Or super-genius brainpower?

Or supermodel looks?

Or just plain luck?

Fortunately, it doesn't require any of the above.

The answer is easy to understand using a simple concept I came up with. It combines two life-changing ideas top performers have known about for years.

I call it 5AVG/TOP5.

What does that mean?

First, let's look at TOP5. Back in the 1950s, the Social Security Administration of America were looking at the retirement statistics. They looked at people who started out at the exact same income at age 25. Then they saw where those people ended up 40 years later at retirement age.

* * *

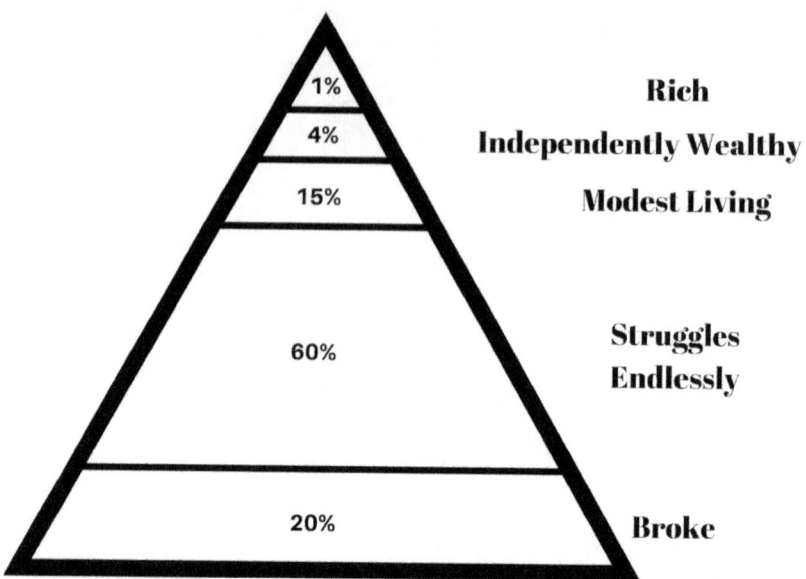

Fig. 2. Where people end up after 40-years when starting from the same income. A study from the Social Security Administration of America.

It turned out the bottom 80% who were still living ranged from barely paying the bills to flat out broke.

The top 20% have a little money, but they still have to compromise between purchases. And some of them were still working too.

The top 5% were financially independent. They could afford to live the life they wanted to live without going overboard.

And the top 1% were very wealthy. They could live a luxurious life while being financially independent.

Now remember, they all started from the same place... the same income level. It's not like they were already rich or poor when they started out. They were all at the same income level.

They repeated the study again and again over the years. They completed the latest one in 2014.

Now how have those statistics changed over the past 60 years?

The answer is they haven't. The 1%/4%/15%/80% divisions were all exactly the same. One difference was more people ended up broke instead of dead. They could thank the higher average life expectancy for that.

Total Money Income of Aged Units

Table 3.A1
Percentage distribution, by marital status and age, 2014

Aged unit income (dollars)	Aged 55-61	Aged 62-64	Aged 65 or older				
			Total	65-69	70-74	75-79	80 or older
			All units				
Total percent	100.0	100.0	100.0	100.0	100.0	100.0	100.0
Less than 1,000	6.2	4.6	3.7	3.6	3.1	3.7	4.3
1,000-1,999	0.7	0.6	0.3	0.2	0.4	0.4	0.4
2,000-2,999	0.4	0.4	0.4	0.3	0.1	0.5	0.5
3,000-3,999	0.4	0.6	0.3	0.2	0.2	0.3	0.3
4,000-4,999	0.4	0.6	0.5	0.4	0.5	0.4	0.6
5,000-5,999	0.5	0.5	0.4	0.2	0.5	0.6	0.4
6,000-6,999	0.5	0.6	0.9	0.7	0.8	0.8	1.2
7,000-7,999	0.7	0.6	1.1	0.9	0.9	1.0	1.6
8,000-8,999	2.1	1.6	1.7	1.4	1.5	2.0	2.0
9,000-9,999	1.6	1.5	2.1	1.8	1.8	2.1	2.6
10,000-10,999	1.8	2.2	2.5	2.1	2.3	2.8	3.0
11,000-11,999	1.0	1.4	2.1	1.8	1.6	2.5	2.6
12,000-12,999	1.0	1.8	2.4	1.9	1.8	2.4	3.4
13,000-13,999	1.0	1.6	2.5	2.0	2.0	2.5	3.5
14,000-14,999	1.0	1.6	2.4	1.6	2.2	2.3	3.4
15,000-19,999	4.6	6.8	10.7	7.5	9.7	11.8	14.8
20,000-24,999	5.3	5.7	8.4	6.8	7.8	8.0	10.4
25,000-29,999	4.7	4.9	7.2	6.1	7.1	7.9	8.1
30,000-34,999	4.6	5.1	5.8	5.1	6.2	5.9	6.4
35,000-39,999	4.5	5.0	5.2	5.2	5.4	5.0	5.2
40,000-44,999	4.2	3.6	4.2	4.3	5.0	4.6	3.3
45,000-49,999	3.1	3.6	3.7	3.7	4.1	4.5	2.6
50,000-54,999	3.8	3.8	3.3	4.1	2.9	3.3	2.5
55,000-59,999	2.9	2.8	2.8	2.8	3.3	2.9	2.3
60,000-64,999	3.2	2.9	2.8	2.9	3.2	2.3	1.7
65,000-69,999	2.7	2.6	2.1	2.5	2.5	2.1	1.4
70,000-74,999	3.0	2.9	2.0	2.5	2.2	1.5	1.6
75,000-99,999	10.7	10.2	6.9	9.5	7.4	5.9	4.0
100,000-149,999	12.1	10.6	6.7	9.8	7.1	5.5	3.6
150,000-199,999	5.5	4.5	2.6	3.8	3.3	1.8	1.1
200,000 or more	5.9	5.0	2.6	4.2	2.9	2.1	0.9
Median income (dollars)	49,464	42,774	30,193	40,013	34,704	28,223	22,232
Number (thousands)	21,315	7,673	34,814	11,056	8,053	6,072	9,434

(Continued)

Fig. 3. The Social Security Administration stats don't change throughout the decades, because we don't change. Income of the Population 55 or Older, 2014 (released April 2016)

All the new technology abilities and financial opportunities didn't make any difference. Compared to the 1950s, it's easier than ever before to start a business, learn new skills, and sell and ship things. You can sell items online instantly without having to wait for the mail. You don't even need a physical store to sell your goods. There are new income opportunities, like being an influencer or guru on YouTube or social media.

You don't even need to trek to the library to learn something; we have everything at our fingertips. We are clicks away from getting whatever information or knowledge we want. And you can even get a lot of it in the form of video on YouTube. You can search how to do this, how to do that, and you'll get videos explaining and walking you through the answer.

We're in the information age. We can do whatever we want. And it's easier than ever to start a business and sell and make money.

Yet how did those numbers not change?

They don't change, because we don't change.

These patterns exist, these numbers exist, these divisions exist, all throughout our society. And when you take a step back, you'll see they exist not only in income. They also exist throughout various industries and activities and everything in life.

Look at any gym. An IHRSA study found 20% of Americans have a gym membership. Yet only 18% of members actually consistently went to the gym. And of those, only 49.9% used the gym at least twice weekly. That's even less than 5% of the total.

A more popular example might be the US Navy SEALS. Less than 10% of those who want to become a SEAL enough to talk to a recruiter make it all the way to being an active-duty SEAL.

And the percentages are even lower for those who want to become a member of the Delta Force. Only about 10% will make it through the Delta Force screening process. And half of those (5% of the total) won't wash out during the later Operators Training Course (OTC).

Of course the idea also applies to the business world. Venture capitalist Peter Thiel talks about the idea of the 'power law' in his book 'Zero To One.' It's that he not only expects to see one or two companies radically outperform the rest of his portfolio. But he expects them to outperform the rest of his portfolio COMBINED. It's in contrast to a more even distribution of performance as we might tend to expect.

And the percentages work beyond these examples as well. Look at any industry, hobby, etc. You'll see each group generally subdivide into 1%/4%/15%/80% subgroups in terms of results. You can kind of think of it like the 80/20 Pareto Principle, but just applied over and over again. Continually narrowing the group to 20% of the previous group, while noticing the results per member increase.

This is actually not a wholly new idea.

In fact, Socrates was talking about it thousands of years ago in the Platonic dialogue 'Euthydemus' when he said:

"Dear Crito, do you not know that in every profession the inferior sort are numerous and good for nothing, and the good are few and beyond all price: for example, are not gymnastic and rhetoric and money-making and the art of the general, noble arts? ...and do you not see that in each of these arts the many are ridiculous performers?"

The most recent improvement to the idea was the more specific percentage breakdowns.

The earliest record of this idea I've found so far was from the 1926 book 'Secret of the Ages.' It was written by Robert Collier. A study was mentioned in the book by the American Banker's Association. It showed, even before social security, only 5% could live without working at age 65. And 5 out of 6 were living on charity at age 65. That's what they found when they traced 100 men at age 25 then followed them to age 65.

It was the motivational speaker Earl Nightingale who later popularized this idea. Earl referenced the Social Security version of the study. He discussed its implications in his recording "The Strangest Secret." Throughout the years, others have promoted the study. People like the motivational speaker Jim Rohn and the successful copywriter Dan Kennedy.

So we must acknowledge these divisions exist and will continue to exist.

Now, you might wonder: is there some formula to identify the top 5%? Is it because of their genetics or something that happened during childhood? This has been studied over the years, and as far as we can tell, it's a roll of the dice. You either are, or you aren't a top 5 percenter. Though there are a couple of ways to influence this, including "5AVG" (which we will discuss soon).

Even people from those poor ghetto areas... a percentage of them manage to escape it. They rocket themselves out of there and become very successful. Now it was harder for them, but a percentage still do. Again, it's a roll of the dice.

Now, there's another concept you need to be aware of, which is what I like to call "5AVG." And you might have heard this concept before:

"You are the average of the five people you spend the most time with."

Jim Rohn was the first to popularize this idea, and he was right. You might even be nodding your head after hearing it, since it at least rings true.

I mean you don't hang around with people who are the exact opposite of you. That's a rare thing. Even for a spouse, most wouldn't tell others, "Yeah, they're nothing like me. They're rude and obnoxious. It's great."

We generally want to hang around with people who are like us. And by that measure, we are also usually like the people we hang around with.

In fact, there's a supporting study from The New England Journal of Medicine which found you have a:

- 57% INCREASE in your chances of becoming obese if a close friend becomes obese.

- This chance increases your total chances to 171% if the obese close friend in question also considers you a close friend.

- There is also a 40% chance increase among siblings.

- And there's a 37% chance increase if you are married to an obese partner.

- Though importantly, there is no effect among neighbors unless they are also friends.

Now, if you've heard of this idea before, you probably thought to yourself the idea made sense.

But that was it.

Nothing came of it.

It didn't propel you to action, because there was no obvious action to take. And without action, even powerful ideas like this are useless.

But there is still a way to make 5AVG both powerful and actionable. That is to combine it with the idea of the Top 5%, or what I like to call TOP5. Together I like to refer to them as 5AVG/TOP5.

When you understand there's a top 5% in any industry. A percent who are taking consistent action and getting good consistent results. And then there's a bottom-95% who aren't taking action and aren't getting consistent results.

You must take a step back and ask yourself:

"What do I want? And am I spending most of my time with the bottom-95% who aren't where I want to be? Or am I spending most of my time with the 5% who are where I want to be, or beyond?"

Here's one last secret from Earl Nightingale. It's what to do if you aren't able to figure out who the TOP5 are in a group or situation. Look for what the bottom-95% is doing, and DON'T do that.

Don't act like the bottom-95%. Don't talk like they talk. Don't go where they go. Don't specialize in what they specialize in. Throw away the "blame list" they all cling to. Don't blame what they blame. Don't use the excuses they use. Start a new life. That's what success speaker Jim Rohn recommended.

It's an excellent exercise to brainstorm who nearby is TOP5. Are you hanging out with them? Or are you hanging with people who are bottom-95 percenters who aren't progressing toward your goals? And if you are hanging out with bottom-95 percenters, that's likely where you'll end up. As you spend more time with them, you're going to get the same results they're getting, which is no results.

There's a popular Russian expression that applies here: "Only dead fish swim with the stream."

It's especially unproductive to hang out with bottom-95 percenters who are also toxic. Or ones that are frustrating, annoying, or negative. Get them out of your life! This can even apply to customers of yours.

What's a good guideline for when to fire a customer? I like this advice from copywriter Dan Kennedy: "If I wake up three mornings in a row frustrated and thinking of you, and you're not my wife, then you've got to go." I apply this advice with my own clients, and so should you.

Now, you might be thinking, "Are you just telling me to drop all my friends and family?"

Of course not!

See it this way:

1. Identify the people you spend the most time with on a weekly basis. This includes time spent together in person, or by voice or messaging.

2. Count how many hours you spend with each person.

3. Simply reallocate your time investment.

4. Make sure the time you spend with TOP5 people that get you closer to your goals is longer than time spent with people who won't.

That's it.

One effective way of improving your 5AVG is looking for mentors. Many of the greatest thinkers and doers benefitted from mentors. Alexander the Great conquered the world after being mentored by Aristotle, one of the smartest living philosophers. And Aristotle was mentored by Plato, who in turn was mentored by Socrates.

It also applies to the business world. Ross Perot was mentored by Joe Batten. Tony Robbins was mentored by Jim Rohn. Billionaire investor Warren Buffet mentored the founder of Microsoft.

And so on.

How do you a find a mentor to help you grow your business? It's simple, just look for successful business owners and CEOs, especially if they're retired and have more free time. A good place to find some local ones is on LinkedIn. That's because you can manually search for business owners and CEOs using their platform. Try to make sure you have some other things in common outside of business, so that you're not there to just suck their brain or be a fly on the wall. It helps if you share interests like golf, hobbies, literature, or other activities. Make finding mentors a part of your effort to improve your 5AVG.

If you're finding it hard to locate and network with TOP5 people in your industry, there's another option. You could join coaching programs in your industry with proven results. Use them to connect with like-minded people who are taking action to ascend higher.

And if you somehow still can't find a coaching group for your industry (or one that you can afford right now) then there's a last resort. You can search for local meetup groups that are ideally at least success-focused. It'd be even better if they were related to your industry. Then check out the group. Try to provide value as you try to find the 5% who are already succeeding (and not just talking about it). It might be only one person. That's fine. At least it's a start.

Who you spend time with is who you become.

Without reading further, you could apply the time-auditing exercise alone and be well on your way to your goals. (Though you'll find it valuable to continue, as I have some ideas that will help you succeed bigger, sooner, and more easily.)

A simple example might be a contractor in the trades. They might find it valuable hanging out with some current or retired owners of a TOP5 electrical contracting business. They might learn at that level almost every TOP5 trade business is promoting yearly maintenance packages to residential clients.

Not only because it increases the average value of each customer. And not only because it's a great way to generate additional referrals and build loyalty. But also because they've found the residential customers love it and find these packages valuable for peace of mind.

And other valuable ideas can be learned from your TOP5 group via discussion. Sometimes practically through osmosis... just by having them in your life.

This isn't rocket science. Anyone can do it.

One of the best aspects of 5AVG/TOP5 is it's one of the only ways to make LASTING changes. As opposed to just reading about something you want to change and not being able to make new positive habits stick, like most people fail with.

Author B.J. Fogg mentions the only other few ways to make lasting change in his book 'Tiny Habits.' Ways like change of environment, having an epiphany, or gradual baby-stepped habits.

But changing your peer group is more impactful and lasting than those other ways. That's because it harnesses your "comfort zone" more than those more common ways. We'll go deeper into this in a little bit.

You now know the secret of the Top 5% and how this fact can help steer you toward success. Especially when you combine it with the idea of 5AVG.

Next, I must show you the highest human "need." Both how it can help you, and how it could hold you back if you don't change it.

Exercise:

1. Write down the five people you spend the most time with outside of your immediate family ("love your family, choose your peer group").

2. Write down the five nearest people you know of who are TOP5 in terms of where you want to be success-wise in your field or activity. Whether in business, career, sports, hobbies, etc. ie. TOP5: entrepreneurs, coworkers, tennis players, fishermen, etc.

3. Cross out any people you spend time with who are obviously toxic or negative influences on your life. Get them out. If one's someone you work with, then change desks or change jobs. There are no real restrictions.

4. Brainstorm ways to introduce yourself to your TOP5 list members and provide value to them. Ask, "How can I bring

more value into their lives?" ie. It's hard to beat asking to buy them lunch or dinner to pick their brain. You can then be straight up with them about the idea of 5AVG/TOP5. They'd be glad to answer questions about what steps they took to get their current results. Everyone likes to tell their story. And they'll let you know what daily actions they're taking that the 95% aren't. Bonus: if they like you, they'll be more likely to introduce you to their friends and any groups they are a part of, who are also most likely TOP5. It all starts with this.

5. Find ways to spend more and more time with the TOP5 list than you do with the current list. You don't have to completely drop your current list from your life (unless they are all toxic influences). You need to spend more time with your TOP5 list members to help speed up your progress into the results you desire.

6. Once a week, do a time audit of the 10 people you spent the most time with. That can include in-person, on the phone, or even just messaging. Write down each person and add up how much time you spent on them over the week. Then order them from longest to shortest. Look over this ordering. If the five people you invested the most time on include people who aren't TOP5, brainstorm both ways to invest less time in them. Then brainstorm ways to invest more time into finding and networking and communicating with other TOP5 people. That which is measured, improves.

CHAPTER THREE

Your Highest Need - How It Can Help Or Hold You Back

Now, I want to touch upon the most fundamental human need and human desire.

Have you ever heard of Maslow's 'Hierarchy of Needs'? It's supposedly a pyramid ranking of fundamental human needs, with the most needed at the bottom of the pyramid. In Abraham Maslow's case, he would consider the physical needs like food, water, shelter, and security to be the most needed.

And he's dead wrong. I'm going to prove it to you right now.

* * *

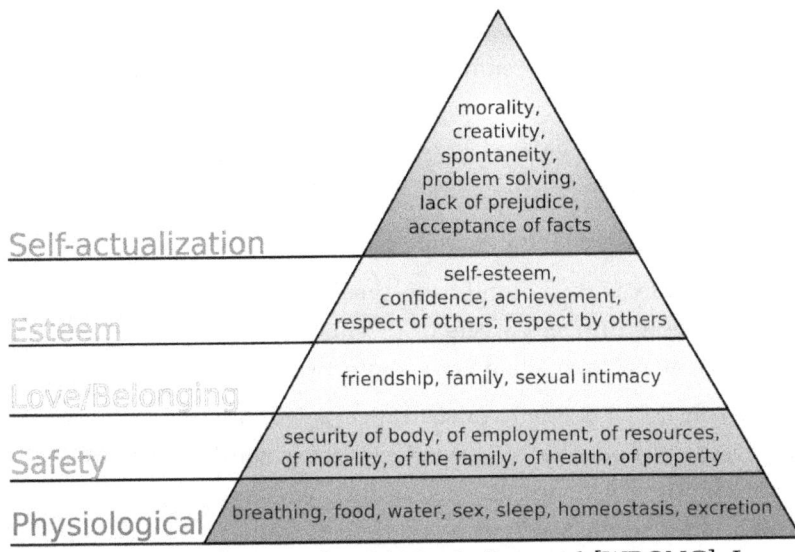

Fig. 4. Maslow's Hierarchy Of Needs Pyramid [WRONG]. Image Credit: J. Finkelstein

There's one higher need that surpasses all.

It's your need to remain in your comfort zone.

You might think that doesn't make any sense. I'll give you an example to prove it. Imagine a person is having a heart attack at a restaurant. Most people would rather try to minimize embarrassment in that situation. They'd prioritize that over getting the maximum amount of medical attention to help save their life. They'd risk death over not making a scene.

Dingy bars that clean up and adjust prices tend to lose their initial clientele.

Golfers tend to maintain their average. If they start a round above average, they'll average out by the final hole. The same applies if they start a round more poorly than usual. They'll again tend to average out by the final hole.

It doesn't matter if there's a good change or a bad change, they'll readjust to move back.

Other people might have a sort of 'financial thermostat' set to a certain level. They will try to lose money if they're doing too well.

And they'll try to make more money if they're not doing well enough. At least that assumes they won't ever try to change their comfort zones.

So we're going to have to throw out Maslow's invalid hierarchy of needs pyramid.

We must create a new pyramid.

And to start with, it won't have "needs." That's because in reality there are only different levels of "wants." And the most powerful "want" of all is to remain in your comfort zone.

So with that, I present you with the new and improved pyramid of "Fraser's Hierarchy of Wants." 95% of it consists of "staying in your comfort zone" and the rest of the items are too small even to read, so they're whatever you want them to be.

Fig. 5. Fraser's Hierarchy Of Wants Pyramid.

Does that make sense? Does that ring true? I'm sure you can imagine other scenarios where the need to remain in your comfort zone trumps all other needs.

I first heard this idea from the late and great copywriter, Gary

Halbert.

The scientific term for comfort zone is "homeostasis." It refers to our tendency to seek stability. Our body prefers stability. This applies to maintaining body temperature, blood pressure, heart rate, blood sugar levels, weight, sleep cycle, and beyond.

Even our individual cells like stability too. That includes maintaining water levels, balance of positive and negative ions, which molecules enter and exit the cell membrane, and so on.

So is it any stretch to believe we have a powerful mental desire for homeostasis as well?

And it goes beyond the previous mental examples. You must understand people want to remain in their comfort zones. This also applies to the idea of money and success.

If someone's been told their whole lives by their parents and peer group they're nothing. Told that they're not going to make anything of themselves, or they're going to be unsuccessful. ie. "We were always poor, our ancestors were poor, so we're always going to be poor." Then that's their comfort zone. It might not be a happy comfort zone, but they haven't died from it, so they might as well remain within it.

And the way to get out of it, especially financially, is to acknowledge success is possible. And acknowledge you deserve success.

We can tie that into 5AVG/TOP5. The motivational speaker Tony Robbins said: "You're the average of the expectations of your peer group."

I will go further and say, "You're the average of the comfort zones of your peer group."

It's why it's sometimes difficult to break away from your peer group. Like how it's hard for a crab to escape a bucket of other crabs without them clawing and pulling it back in.

That's your destiny.

* * *

Fig. 6. An analogy for trying to escape the comfort zones of your peers. Image Credit: W.carter

It's sad because they prevent you from succeeding. And they might not even be doing it consciously. It's their comfort zones because they're comfortable.

An unpleasant success principle Dan Kennedy likes to use is, "You are exactly where you really want to be." So you must first change where you really want to be at a deep internal level if you wish ever to escape it. That's what the next few chapters will help you do.

So what is a comfort zone?

It's the beliefs, actions, and habits that have been conditioned into your mind and biology. You subconsciously believe: "This has been working so far, let's not do anything risky. I'm alive, I'm breathing. Just keep doing this. Don't change anything too drastically. And don't change the things around me either. And don't let the people around me change either."

Maybe that's evolution, maybe it's something else. Who knows?

But what it comes down to is the idea "This has been working so far. Let's keep everything the way it is."

That's a problem for you if you want to upgrade to a situation much better than the one you're currently in.

It applies to your peer group and their comfort zones. If you start ascending or are talking about ascending and doing things they don't expect from you. Their comfort zones start to feel a little anxious. They don't want you to change.

They're comfortable with you right where you are right now. And they'll try to prevent you from ascending... maybe not even consciously. They'll try to pull you back down. This is why it's hard for people to ascend; their present peer group's comfort zones hold them back.

Those who've tried dieting in the past might've experienced a "friend" tempting them with "Oh c'mon, try a piece of this. What's a little bite going to hurt?" Or another "friend" might offer a cigarette to someone trying to quit smoking. And so forth.

On the other hand, their comfort zones also don't want you to be in a worse situation than you are in now. If you're feeling more down than usual, they'll want to cheer you up. If you're more sick than usual, they'll want you to be healthy. And that's why it's hard to separate yourself from your peer group. When you're feeling unwell, the comfort zones of your peer group want to help bring you back up to where you were before.

But then the problem is they won't only pull you up, they'll also pull you down.

That's why you must upgrade your peer group. You must get one where everyone's comfort zone includes taking action and ascending toward their goals. A peer group where they all believe success is possible, and they deserve success. This is what TOP5 people do.

When you understand this... and when you combine your comfort zone and your peer groups' comfort zones with 5AVG/TOP5... you can then understand the great importance of upgrading your peer group to the TOP5 who are succeeding.

Now maybe you are succeeding right now. Perhaps you had a lucky dice roll. You are right now in a TOP5 peer group that is taking action and getting closer to their goals (not just talking about it). Great!

In that case just keep these lessons in mind as you continue to take action. Ascend and seek out even more successful people to surround yourself with. Keep this up until you make it all the way to the top with your highest desired result. Getting great consistent results beyond 95% of the other people with similar goals. Keep rocketing higher and higher. Maybe the CEO or owner of a Fortune 500 company? Perhaps a gold medalist? Maybe an early and wealthy retirement? Perhaps the founder of a very impactful charity? And so on.

So if you are already implementing 5AVG/TOP5, congratulations. Otherwise, that's what you'll want to implement. You'll want to surround yourself with people who've already achieved your goal or beyond. Or at least people who have ascended higher than you are at present.

Some might be skeptical they can even change their comfort zone. They might have tried hard in the past, but just snapped right back to where they were before. This is likely for one of two reasons. Either their current peer group pulled them back immediately or gradually, or they tried to stretch their comfort zone too far too fast.

The second reason is very common. If you stretch your comfort zone too far, it's very likely to snap right back. So usually the best way to change your comfort zone involves gradual stretching of it over time. This same idea equally applies to successfully building habits that last.

But there are two exceptions that allow you to stretch your comfort zone very far without snapping back. The first is a drastic change of your environment. ie. Moving to another city. And the second exception is… changing your peer group. As you can see, I'm giving you the tools for maximum change and lasting change.

So again, do the exercises in the previous chapter. What people do you spend most of your time with now? Ask yourself, "Where am I in their comfort zone?" And ask yourself what nearby people are TOP5? What is their comfort zone?

Then immediately take massive action and contact these people to hang out with them. Buy them lunch, buy them dinner, or brainstorm other ways you think you can provide them value. Become a part of their lives (and their comfort zones).

And if there are people around you with toxic or negative comfort zones, then drop them now.

You must do this to help get the results you want. Do it for yourself and for your family.

Fulfill your destiny and get what you want out of life.

You've now identified any problem areas in your comfort zone that might hold you back from the success you deserve. And you have a plan to make your new comfort zone one of deserved success.

In fact, I can now reveal the secret most successful people use to get results and get motivated. It's an *unusual* form of goal setting paired with a supporting framework for lasting change.

Now you're likely thinking, "Well, I've tried goal setting in the past. I know people who've tried it. It didn't seem to help much."

You might be right. And the problem is the way it was done.

Most people are unaware of the fact there are many ways to set goals.

If you look at the top performers, they set goals in a very different way than most people. That's what I want to give you first in this book. I want you to have the goal-setting method top performers in their industry use. It helps get them maximum results, real results, consistent results, and lasting results. To improve their lives and get what they want.

I will go further into that throughout this first part of the book.

Next, you're going to see a more specific vision of exactly what you want out of life.

Exercise:

1. Take a step back and write down any negative parts of your comfort zone that might be holding you back. It could be comfortable being: poor, unsuccessful, at an unhealthy weight, unhappy, clumsy, lonely, etc.

2. Now, write down the new positive aspects of the new comfort zone you wish to have. Write down each of them in this format: "X is possible, and I deserve X." ie. "Success is possible, and I deserve success." "Happiness is possible, and I deserve happiness." And so on. You'll learn how to enact these changes in the next chapter.

CHAPTER FOUR

What Do You Really Want?

As I mentioned before, when it comes to goal setting, the TOP5 do it differently.

They don't just write down a list of what they want. Now that's actually more than most people do. But at the same time, let's improve it by taking it a bit further.

First, let's get the obvious out of the way and not set goals that are impossibly challenging. This is supported by a 2009 Harvard Business study on "Goals Gone Wild." It found goals that were set too high and unrealistic actually hurt overall performance and motivation. So at least set goals that are realistically attainable.

On the other hand, you don't want to set goals that are too easy or general. Goals like "I will try my best at this task" do almost nothing to improve performance. Edwin Locke found this in his 1968 study at Harvard on the specific positive results of goals. Locke found that hard, yet attainable goals drove performance better than easy goals.

Next, you could be SPECIFIC about what you want. Instead of wanting to be "happy" in general, you can specify that you want to "be happy traveling the world in early retirement." Or specify "be happy living in a mansion with four healthy children" or whatever else you might want.

Locke found specific hard goals improved performance more than vaguely-worded goals. Being specific helps make the goal more concrete and targeted. The more specific you are, the easier it will be to come up with steps to get you there. And it also makes goals feel more real and attainable.

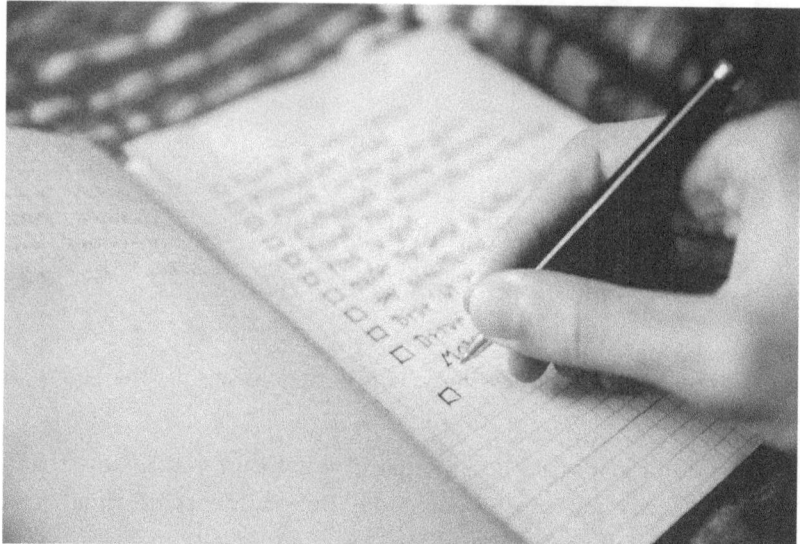

Fig. 7. The best argument for writing down your goals is the bottom 95% don't. Image Credit: StockSnap

Even better: specify when you expect to reach each goal. Do that by specifying a realistic timeframe. ie. "I want to achieve this goal by this date." This helps frame your goals as more concrete and attainable. As long as the timeframe is within the realm of possibility.

On the other hand, a timeline can hinder progress if it's not ambitious enough. In that case, a non-specific "as soon as possible" would be better. Either way, the important thing is your timeline should be ambitious, yet again, still within the realm of possibility.

But is there an even better way beyond combining a goal and a date? How about integrating a plan of action? What are the steps you need to take to achieve each goal? You might not know all the steps, but you can at least write the steps you're confident of at the moment.

Now you have laid out a realistic plan and timeframe for getting what you want. That's a solid form of goal setting. That's more than the vast majority of people do.

Yet the TOP5 still have a better way.

It can be even more beneficial for you.

It can help you realize what you want more specifically.

It can help inspire you with new micro-steps and paths to get you closer to each goal.

And it can do all this daily; generating inspiration and reinforcing action.

So the TOP5 are already hanging out with other TOP5 people in their peer group. And they're learning the steps others took to get where they are. This can help them figure out what steps they need to take to reach their goals.

In addition, the TOP5 set goals by turning their list of goals into declarations and visualizations they review DAILY.

I will go into this further, but first, let's start by actually generating you a list of goals. I got these exercise ideas from the late success writer Joe Karbo. He came up with the best goal-setting techniques back in the 1970's, and they have yet to be improved upon. He named it "Dyna/Psyc," as in "dynamic psychology." Most top producers use a close variation of this method. And there have been no major improvements found in over 40 years.

Top people in the field of sales all swore by it. People like Gary Halbert, Gary Bencivenga, John Carlton, and Ben Suarez. Ben actually dedicated an entire chapter to praising this method in his book. In it, he explained how he used the method to gross more than $120 million the previous year.

Tony Robbins used a very similar system for setting goals.

Even Jordan Belfort, the former "Wolf of Wall Street," used an almost identical goal-setting method. He used it to train and inspire sales teams he was hired to consult.

The closest variation that would loosely count as a "modern" update to this system is something called OKR. It stands for Objectives and Key Results. It's what Google employees use to effectively set out and track their projects. It's basically the same as Karbo's method. The only notable difference is OKRs incorporate "stretch goals." This is where you set out the most optimistic ideal goals possible, but would be very difficult to actually reach. You should be doing this anyway with all your goals.

The further you reach, the greater your grasp (AKA: results).

The only other notable OKR difference is the emphasis on regularly tracking your goals, and adjusting them along the way. You'll see next chapter how not only does the Karbo method account for this, it actually does it at an even higher frequency than Google.

I'm all for tracking your goals. It's important to know you're on the right track, as this Steven Covey quote illustrates:

"If the ladder is not leaning against the right wall, every step we take just gets us to the wrong place faster."

I have one last bonus tip for adding a kinesthetic (learning via touch) layer to your goal setting. I got this tip from the success speaker Bob Proctor. And Bob got it from Earl Nightingale, his mentor. It involves creating a "Goal Card" with your most important short-term goal written on it. Also write down the date you want to reach the goal.

Keep this Goal Card in your pocket every day. Then whenever you reach for your keys, wallet, or phone, you will feel the card and be reminded kinaesthetically of your goal. You will get renewed and reinforced vigor to ensure you're taking every action possible to get closer to it. It will also help inspire you with new steps you can take to reach your goal sooner.

We will go further into Joe Karbo's valuable method in the next chapter. First, complete the exercises below to generate and refine your list of goals.

<u>WARNING!</u>

* * *

Don't tell anyone about your list of goals, hopes for the future, or daily steps! The only exception is if someone else is taking these steps with you, like an "accountability buddy." This is most important early on. Your mind must do everything it can to prevent the invasion of doubt, no matter how small, from both yourself and especially from other people. Give yourself a chance to fulfill these goals. Once you start reaching each goal, people will be asking for advice. Then you can talk. Don't take any chances before that.

You now have a better and more specific vision of what you want out of life.

Next, we'll discuss a powerful way to supercharge your journey toward realizing this vision.

"Are you pleased with your present place in the world? If your answer is yes, what's your next port of call? If your answer is no, what are you going to do about it?"

— Earl Nightingale

Exercise:

1. In the following steps, you will build and revise your list of goals. This includes things you need now, things you want, and the personality goals you'll need to help get the former goals. In the following chapter, we'll discuss ways to supercharge their effectiveness.

2. Write down a list of things you need RIGHT NOW. ie. Car repair, a new suit, medical insurance, bills paid, dental work, etc. Anything necessary to satisfy your current requirements. Be SPECIFIC.

3. Write down a list of things you want, whether you need them or not. ie. Rolls Royce, $5,000,000 house, 60-foot yacht, original Picasso painting, one-year trip around the world, $1,000,000 a year income, climb Everest, etc. Be SPECIFIC.

4. Write down the personality qualities you need and want. Qualities that will help guarantee your success, get respect, earn friendship, or whatever feelings we want from others. ie. Power to get things done, confidence, be friendlier, be in good health, be more aggressive, more creative, etc. You can also reuse here your desired changes to your comfort zone from the last chapter. Be SPECIFIC.

5. Go over each list item and for each item ask:

    - Is it clear and specific? Is the timeline specific too?

    - Do you really want it? Or would it just sound good to others? Or is it so small that it's easy to achieve, yet not what you really want?

    - Does this goal contradict any other goal? ie. Make sure your goal income can support your goal purchases.

    - Would your family support these goals? Talk with them to help make any adjustments.

    - Are they positive goals? Specify things you want, not what you want to rid yourself of. ie. "Get things done" is better than "stop procrastination." And "my fridge is filled with only healthy, yet delicious food" is better than "I don't eat junk food."

    - Is the goal realistic? Has a human ever achieved it before?

    - Is it lofty enough? Don't put goals that are merely achievable, yet aren't what you truly desire. If you want to think big, then aim big.

    - Have you included all the personality goals necessary to achieve this goal?

    - Is each goal stated as if it's already been accomplished? This is essential, and you'll see why in the next chapter. ie. Instead of writing "I want/need/wish...", write "I have/am/own..."

    - Is each goal preceded by your name? This will help

further reinforce the goal is attainable by you (we want to utilize every drop of potential goal-setting power). Before each goal, write "I, YOUR NAME." ie. "I, Fraser Druet, have..."

6. Bonus: here are some sample positive goals similar to the ones Joe Karbo recommended everyone include in their list in addition to their other goals. At least try them out for a few weeks. You might be surprised how relevant, helpful, and inspiring they can be:

- I, YOUR NAME, am becoming more effective and better able to function without limitation by doing these visualizations twice daily.

- I, YOUR NAME, pursue my goals without any negative feelings toward others. I'm well-liked and my success is guaranteed. I feel obliged to help others without needing to tell people about my accomplishments.

- I, YOUR NAME, see myself as successful right NOW. I've thrown away any negative self-perception from my past. I am limitless.

7. Bonus 2: Write a "Goal Card" containing your most important short-term goal. By keeping it in your pocket, you will add another kinesthetic layer of goal reinforcement. Create it this way:

- Cut out a piece of paper the size of a business card. Or use a blank index card

- Write "MY GOAL" at the top. And beside it put the date you want to reach this goal by.

- Below it, write "I, YOUR NAME, am so happy and grateful now that..." and follow it with your most important short-term goal

- Wrap your card with clear tape. Packing tape is good. You could also laminate it. This is important to keep it safe over weeks or months in your pocket with keys, wallet, phone, etc.

- Put it in your pocket every morning. That's it

- Make a new Goal Card after you achieve each goal

8. Now you have your list of goals. In the next chapter, we'll discuss how the TOP5 supercharge their results from their goals.

CHAPTER FIVE

The TOP5 Secret to Accelerate Your Vision

You should now have a nice refined list of goals. If not, then go back and follow the exercises to create your list. This is of paramount importance.

The fact that 90 to 95% of people randomly surveyed have never written down their goals is maybe the best argument for doing it. And a 2020 study by Gail Matthews found those with written goals were 50.46% more likely to achieve them than those with unwritten goals. So go do it.

In this chapter, we are going to act like a TOP5 percenter and supercharge the effectiveness of your list of goals. We'll do this by harnessing the power of visualization.

You're likely reading this book right now while sitting and relaxed. So you're in a perfect position to practice this new goal-setting method and begin to see its potential for yourself.

Follow these steps, and then I will explain how it all works:

1. Sit relaxed somewhere comfortable with your list of goals.

2. Read the first goal; aloud if possible, silently while moving your lips if not.

3. Close your eyes, and visualize that goal completely in your mind. SEE the mansion, the happiness, the traveling, the yacht, the specific success, etc. Walk around your mansion,

look in the mirror at your smile, gaze at the distant ocean sunrise from your yacht, feel that $50,000 commission check in your hands, etc.

4.   Rinse and repeat with each remaining goal.

5.   Do this twice daily to maximize its impact.

6.   Add, tweak, and remove goals as you are inspired with new ideas and accomplish your current goals.

Now that is how a TOP5 person harnesses goal setting.

It's basically supercharging your goal-setting effectiveness by turning them into affirmations with the power of visualizations. Now, there might be some who are skeptical of affirmations. I myself was skeptical at first. But as I dug into the scientific underpinnings of it and practiced it myself, I gradually saw the benefits.

For instance, a 2014 study by Cohen & Sherman found our self-identity is flexible and can be shaped by affirmations. That is to say, instead of seeing yourself in just one "fixed" way, such as a "teacher" or a "daughter," our self-identity is already flexible even without affirmations. So affirmations just help shift our self-identities into the most positive and optimal ones for each situation.

A 1969 study by Aronson found this is good because we can then be more adaptable and competent in each situation. This improves our overall performance and helps us reach our desired results more quickly.

We even find evidence of positive changes from affirmations in the brain. A 2016 study by Cascio found using MRI scanning certain neural pathways are increased when people practice positive affirmations. Specifically, the ventromedial prefrontal cortex becomes more active. It's involved with processing information related to the self and positive valuation.

This showed its value in a 2015 study by Falk. They were trying to see if affirmations could help people better process a diagnosis of cancer and otherwise-threatening messages.

* * *

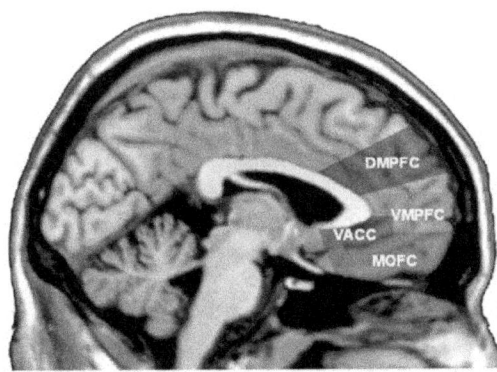

DMPFC (BA 9, 32): Certainty in evaluations.

VMPFC (BA 10, 32): Socioemotional significance or cognitive quality of information?

VACC (BA 25): Sensitivity to information based on its potential to fulfill motivation.

MOFC (BA 11, 12): Shifts in evaluation standards under threat.

Fig. 8. The VMPFC (ventromedial prefrontal cortex) becomes more active when practicing positive affirmations. Image Credit: Flagan T and Beer JS

They used functional magnetic resonance imaging to see at a neurological level what happens when people do positive affirmations. They found people are better able to handle threatening problems that life throws at them. They were better able to handle this information, and also better able to see the value in it to help their future decisions.

There are many studies supporting the various benefits of affirmations. A 2017 study by Layous found they can reduce GPA decline in college students. A 2014 study by Cooke found affirmations can help those increase their physical activity. In 2012, Logel & Cohen did a study that found affirmations can help us receive stressful messages more effectively. A 2015 study by Critcher & Dunning found affirmations can help reduce unhealthy stress. A 2001 study from Weisenfeld found affirmations can help reduce persistent negative thoughts and stress. And a 2008 study from Epton & Harris found they can even help people eat more fruit and vegetables. These are just a handful of the supporting studies I found.

Though these are just benefits of affirmations alone. We haven't even begun to scratch the surface of how much more powerful they can be made with visualization.

Depending on how many goals you've set and how long you

visualize each goal, this process could take only 2 to 20 minutes. ie. For a list of 15 goals visualized for 20 seconds each, it would take only 5 minutes.

Be aware the most critical step in this process is the actual visualization of each goal. Actually SEEING it in your mind as if you've already accomplished it. Why is that? And how does this process work to benefit you?

What this process is actually doing is harnessing the power of your subconscious mind. It's using it to generate inspiration, action, and habit; all in a consistent programmed way. What a mouthful.

I'll make it simpler. Have you ever tried to remember something, but couldn't, and then a couple days later it popped into your mind out of the blue? I'm sure you have.

Next, have you ever worked hard on a problem or tried to figure something out, looking for an answer? And then sometime later, likely when you weren't working on it, the answer popped into your head out of the blue? Maybe you were in the shower or brushing your teeth, or going for a walk? Or were otherwise doing something unrelated to finding the solution? I'm sure you have.

Everyone has this happen to them. Everyone has this ability.

What was happening in both cases was, unbeknownst to you, you were feeding your subconscious with a problem to solve. Whether it was a difficult problem to solve, or even just trying to remember something you forgot. Your subconscious heard your request and got to work. Then when it was finished, it just popped the answer into your stream of conscious thought. That was likely when your conscious mind was occupied with something unrelated.

You must understand your subconscious mind is at least as powerful as your conscious mind. Perhaps many times more powerful. It is a giant neural network of pattern recognition and connectivity. It is connecting ideas together to generate answers and inspiration.

Bob Nease explored this vast difference in his book 'The Power of Fifty Bits.' He wrote, "fifty bits refers to a startling statistic: of the ten million bits of information our brains process each second, only fifty bits are devoted to conscious thought."

Our modern neural network computer systems try to replicate the structure of our mind. Though all of them combined cannot match the power of a single human subconscious mind. At least not yet.

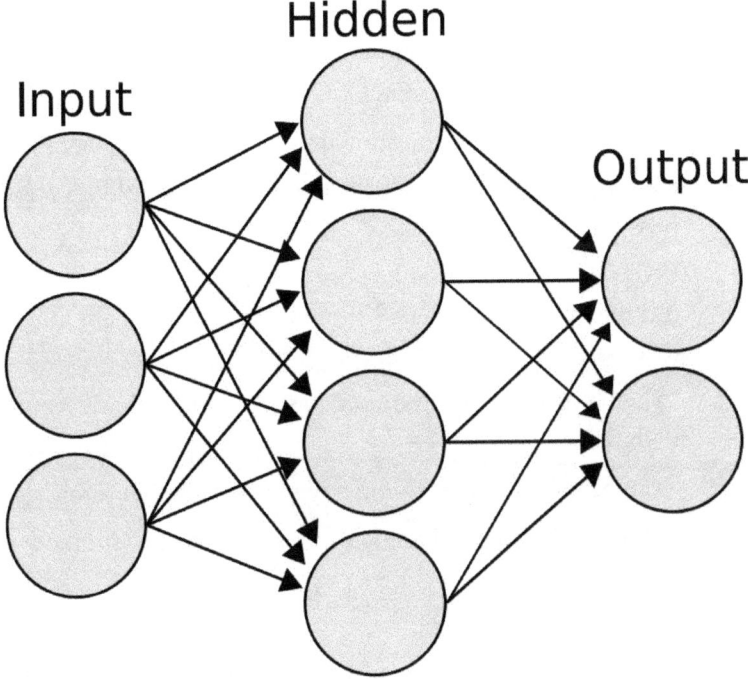

Fig. 9. Artificial Neural Network diagram. Image Credit: Cburnett

Okay, that sounds neat, but what does this have to do with goal setting and visualizations?

Well, when you are doing your daily goal visualizations, what you are really doing is feeding this vision into your subconscious. Remember, your subconscious sees everything you see, both in reality and in your mind.

So when you feed it these visualizations, you are also feeding it the achieved goal. That's why I made you write each goal as having already been achieved. So your subconscious is fed these achieved visions. And it knows they haven't yet been realized, so it gets to work trying to make your achieved goals REAL.

It's as if your subconscious has been given a problem to be solved. In this case, the problem is: "Here is a possible reality, how can I help make it my reality?" Then your subconscious gets to work on getting you closer to this reality. It does this by periodically feeding you inspiration. Usually in the form of things you can do and steps you can take to get you closer and closer to realizing each goal. Valuable steps you or other people might not have considered.

Here are some example inspirational steps you might generate:

- "Maybe I should contact this person, they would be a good prospect for my business…"
- "Who lives nearby that has been to the top of Everest? How did they prepare? Maybe I should offer to buy them lunch to discuss…"
- "Maybe this would be a good person to joint venture with…"
- "Maybe I should start doing oxygen-deprivation training…"
- "Maybe this is a good angle I should be using to promote my business…"
- Etc.

Then all that's left is for you to take massive action and follow each step as it's fed to you by your subconscious.

It also helps condition your subconscious into seeing yourself as the successful person from the visions you feed it. And as your subconscious mind starts to see yourself that way, then your conscious mind will as well.

So you aren't only generating inspiration, you are also BECOMING more like someone who achieves the goals you've set out to do. You are BECOMING more like someone who cashes $50,000 checks. You are BECOMING more like someone who has climbed Everest. And so on with your own goals.

The Buddha quote, "We are what we think about" applies here. (I prefer "We are what we do," which I'll cover later).

You'll want to do these visualizations twice daily. Once in the morning. This will help prime your subconscious to work at maximum capacity for the rest of the day. And once right before bed. This will help your subconscious work while you sleep.

Remember, while your conscious mind is asleep, your subconscious mind is working away at whatever you fed it. So you might as well feed it visions it can help make real.

Also the longer and more detailed you make your visualizations, the more powerful your results will be.

And it's not only successful business people who profit from these visualization techniques. Athletes enjoy them too.

Look at Olympic gold-medalist Michael Phelps. His swimming coach trained him to "play a videotape" in his mind of him completing a perfect swim. With every single molecule of his body moving precisely where it should at the exact time it should to complete the swim as quickly as possible.

His coach would then have Michael "play the tape" in his mind many times daily. Including WHILE ACTUALLY SWIMMING. This helped him condition his actual swimming performance. He could replicate the perfect movements he was performing in his perfect visualized swim.

One thing you might do to help out this process is periodic assessments of your current goals. Sort of like how Google employees will regularly track and iterate their OKR-style goals. Pick a timeframe to take a step back and assess your goals. Weekly is best, but monthly is fine too. Just schedule a regular repeating time to ask yourself questions like:

- How are your vision goals coming along?
- Is there anything slowing down your progress?
- What do you need to do to accelerate progress for each goal?
- How do you need to grow to achieve your grand vision?

Merely asking yourself these questions will help inspire future inspiration from your subconscious. Though when you do get some good answers, you can use them to adjust your goals and vision along the way.

One last way to make these visualizations more impactful and effective is to change how they look, sound, and feel in your mind. I got this idea from motivational speaker Tony Robbins. I've added it to the exercise steps below. Try it. You'll be surprised how much of a positive difference they can make.

I've laid out the fundamentals of this method. You can find more information on this method by reading Joe Karbo's book "The Lazy Man's Way To Riches." Now I promise you when I first heard that title, my brain immediately yelled "garbage scam book title." I looked for every excuse not to read it. But luckily I already knew many top business owners gave this method their highest recommendation, so I pressed on. And I'm happy to have found and applied its treasures.

Below are some exercises to help turn this goal-setting and visualization process into an easy SYSTEM. You can use it daily to progress toward your goals.

You now have a great strategy and plan for getting what you want. And you have a powerful process to help illuminate the steps along the way. But not everyone makes it happen.

Next, we'll be discussing the main reason some people don't succeed with this method. And I'll share a secret 10-second tip to help step toward success every day.

Exercise:

1.   First, here's a recap of how to get the most out of these visualizations:

- Sit relaxed somewhere comfortable with your list of goals.

- Read the first goal; aloud if possible, silently while moving your lips if not.

- Close your eyes, and visualize that goal completely in your mind. SEE the mansion, the happiness, the traveling, the yacht, the specific success, etc. Walk around your mansion, look in the mirror at your smile, gaze at the distant ocean sunrise from your yacht, feel that $50,000 commission check in your hands, etc.

- Rinse and repeat with each remaining goal.

- Do this twice daily to maximize its impact.

- Add, tweak, and remove goals as you are inspired with new ideas and accomplish your current goals.

2. Now, divide a piece of 8.5 "x11" paper into 30 rows with 2 columns each.

3. Number each row from 1 to 30. These will represent the next 30 days, starting with your current day.

4. Name the left column "AM" and the right column "PM."

5. This will be your reminder and enforcer of your twice-daily visualizations. I recommend putting it on your pillow after doing your morning visualizations (and crossing off the AM column for that day). At night right before bed, after doing your nightly visualizations (and crossing off the PM column for that day), place it somewhere on top of something you interact with before you do your morning visualizations. This could be:

- On top of your phone.

- Rolled up and sticking out of a shoe.

- On a chair you usually sit on in the morning.

- Etc. (Just make sure it's in the way, so you're forced to touch and interact with it)

6. Bonus: you can even add a reminder in the form of a sticky note on your bathroom mirror. This can be a secondary reminder for both the AM and PM affirmations, just in case.

7. If you haven't already done so, do your first round of visualizations right now and check off the first AM box (or PM if it's now your bedtime).

8. Then for the next 30 days check off every single AM and PM box to reinforce these visualizations until they're habitual. This will maximize their effectiveness and get you closer than ever before to your goals.

9. Going forward, I'd even recommend using a similar reminder to ensure twice daily compliance. This could be an index card on your bed, or even the marked-up original piece of paper. Then you will never fall out of this valuable habit.

10. Bonus 2: Try incorporating visual, audio, and kinesthetic attributes into each visualization to help make them feel even more powerful and effective. ie.

    -   Make the scene look bigger and brighter in your mind.

    -   Raise the volume of the voices or sounds you hear. Give them more bass, more rhythm, a change in timbre. Make them more affirmative and stronger.

    -   Make the vision feel warmer and softer and smoother.

CHAPTER SIX

Where People Go Wrong: The Secret To Getting Results

So you have a good understanding of 5AVG/TOP5 and your comfort zone. You have a list of goals.

You have the greatest method for achieving them using visualizations and your subconscious.

And you have a 30+ day plan of action for maximizing their effectiveness.

How could this possibly not work?

The answer is simple: it's because when it came to the 30+ day plan of action, no action was taken. And no action was taken toward achieving each goal.

That's one of the big reasons why the 95% are the 95%. They don't take the actions required to escape from their do-nothing peers and ascend to the top.

Positive thinking and positive visualization are great, but ACTION is required to produce results.

I've dedicated this chapter to revealing two ways to help you take action.

First, here's a secret way to immediately start each day with a burst of success from action. Best of all, it takes less than 10 seconds to do, yet few actually do this and harness its motivating power.

What is it?

Simple. Make your bed.

That's it.

It should take less than 10 seconds. I can usually do it in a few seconds now that I've mastered it. And it shouldn't need perfectly angled hospital corners or a dozen pillows to arrange.

So spend 10 seconds making your bed to begin the day with the feeling of accomplishment. This might sound crazy or over-hyped, but do it and see.

Fig. 10. Make your bed. Start your day with success. It takes seconds. Image

Credit: Jazella, Pixabay.

* * *

Why is it so beneficial?

This is one of the reasons militaries emphasize soldiers having well-made beds in the morning. It conditions them to start their day with success too. It will help them feel more prepared to carry that success into the battlefield later.

U.S. Navy Admiral William McRaven, a retired Navy Seal officer, said if you want to change the world, you should start by making your bed. He even dedicated a book to it titled "Make Your Bed."

This powerful action method is even used to help heroin addicts recover. When everything seems to be falling apart in their lives, they can at least start the day with one accomplishment. Over time this will help condition more and more accomplishment throughout the day. Until the day they are finally rehabilitated.

How can you make this habit easy to remember and conditioned into your routine?

It's simple. Put a sticky note on your bathroom mirror at eye-level that reads "Make my bed."

That's it.

Over time you'll condition yourself not to forget until it's a part of you. Until you always start your day with ACTION and accomplishment.

After much practice it now only takes me a few seconds to make my bed. I even do part of it while getting out of bed to save even more time.

Though remember, even if it's easy to do, then it's also easy not to do. That's another reason why the 95% doesn't take action; it's too easy not to.

Now there's still one missing secret ingredient to getting results in anything. I'm going to give you the secret to getting the most out of taking action.

When it comes to it, don't just take action, take MASSIVE action.

If there are 15 different steps you can take right now to get closer to your goals, then don't do one at a time. Do ALL of them simultaneously.

Do as many actions as possible at once.

That's the definition of taking massive action. Look at job hunting.

Winners don't apply to one company at a time, patiently waiting through each interview round before applying elsewhere. Winners apply to ALL prospective companies simultaneously to minimize their time spent job-hunting. Then they can take that same energy and initiative to rapidly advance in their careers too.

So if your goal is to climb Everest, own a Bentley, and ascend to the top of your industry, then don't order a book from someone who climbed Everest and wait. Instead, order ALL the books/DVDs/etc on Everest and similar climbs. AND schedule a test drive with the closest Bentley dealer. AND order all the books and trade journals in your industry to consume and look for patterns the most successful share.

All those actions could be done on the same day. Perhaps even the same hour.

That's how you've got to approach life if you want maximum results as quickly as possible.

Positive thinking and visualizations are a start, but they're not the full answer. Visualization without action is the beginning of delusion. Visualization with action creates miracles.

Now that you're implementing TOP5 goal setting, you should be getting inspired with more and more steps to help you get closer to your goals. So TAKE THEM ALL. Don't wait.

And again, you can prime every day for massive action by making your bed.

Now you're motivated and have a plan to take massive action to get what you want. But I want to touch on one last thing.

In the first chapter, I mentioned that if you weren't where you wanted to be in business or life, it wasn't your fault. That was true. WAS true...

Now things have changed.

Now it merely "wasn't your fault." That's because you've just learned the most effective exercises to identify and realize your vision. You've learned what's been holding you back (and what is still holding back the great majority of people).

You've peeked behind the curtain in Oz.

You've turned around to see the reality of Plato's cave.

You've eaten from the tree of knowledge, and can see your previously comfortable Eden of "It's not my fault" evaporating around you.

And just like waking up from the Matrix... there's no going back.

So in its place, you'll now practice something called "Extreme Ownership." It's based on a leadership philosophy used by the Navy Seals and popularized by the book of the same name. It means from now on you'll recognize that EVERYTHING IS YOUR FAULT.

If you're feeling down because your toxic so-called "friends" are making fun of your vision, then it's YOUR FAULT for not following the 5AVG exercises. Then they'd be kicked to the curb and replaced with TOP5 friends who want you to succeed and realize your vision.

If you feel like being more successful would change you and make you a worse person, then it's YOUR FAULT for not following the Comfort Zone exercises. Then you'd feel at a deep level you deserve success.

If you don't have a clear vision yet nor the steps to achieve it, then it's YOUR FAULT for not doing the Karbo exercises. Then you'd clarify your vision and use daily visualizations to inspire your subconscious. So your subconscious would show you the steps you need to take to help realize your vision.

And if you aren't soon multiplying your customers or leapfrogging your competition, then it's YOUR FAULT for not doing the upcoming exercises.

Though there's a silver lining to everything being your fault. At least everything is now finally in YOUR CONTROL. You control your vision and your destiny. It just takes action.

You now know the importance of taking massive action and how to start your day with action and success. And you've also acknowledged now everything is your fault, but at least you are in control.

In the next part, we'll discuss ways to multiply your customers by reaching and nurturing more of the prospects you're already getting.

Exercise:

1. Make your bed if it's not already made. Try to do it as quickly as possible while still making it look good.

2. Put a sticky note on your bathroom mirror at eye-level and write "Make my bed" on it.

3. Brainstorm a list of all the actions and steps you can take to get closer to your goals. Then take massive action right now and do as many of them as you can.

4. Take "Extreme Ownership" of your life and problems since you are now in control.

PART TWO

MULTIPLY YOUR CUSTOMERS

CHAPTER SEVEN

The 1-Minute Secret To Multiplying Your Conversion Rate

Now that you're motivated with a solid plan of massive action, let's get down to business.

I'm going to let you in on a little-known secret to multiplying your customers for free.

This is no exaggeration.

You can do it by converting more of the prospects, leads, and referrals you're already getting right now. Especially the ones you are already paying for, so you don't have to spend a cent more to multiply your current results.

It works for any source of prospects. From leads generated online to personal referrals from a friend.

And the best part is it takes less than 5 minutes per prospect.

How can you do it? I'm sure you're well aware that to convert a prospect to a customer, you must first REACH them. The vast majority of businesses have trouble converting their leads. That's because they aren't maximizing the amount they actually reach and connect with in the first place.

Especially if you need to reach them on the phone, which you should be using if you're not dealing with insane volume. There is no more effective way of converting prospects than by phone, aside from face-to-face. Below phone in terms of effectiveness is FedEx, then snail mail. Then below a few other sales methods, just below sky-writing in terms of effectiveness, is email. (Note: again, I'm talking about effectiveness here, not efficiency).

So use the phone as much as possible to help conversions. There's a reason most high-ticket sales teams focus on phone sales.

I wanted to find the best practices for maximizing the percent of prospects you reach (and convert). To find out, I read and harvested 48 different industry studies. They are all listed in the back of the book in the appendix.

Fig. 11. The list of 48 industry studies I harvested for this chapter.

Don't worry, we aren't going to go through every study. We're only going to cover the most powerful findings (most of which are from only two of the studies).

The first study we'll look at was commissioned in 2011. It was in regard to what the best practices were to actually reach your leads.

The study was later published in Harvard Business Review (which I'll refer to as HBR from now on).

It was carried out by the company InsideSales. Over three years, they tracked and studied the results of over 100,000 call attempts to over 15,000 leads from six companies.

They learned how some callers were reaching several TIMES more prospects than their peers.

What they found was shocking.

First of all, when it comes to phone response time, on average, most companies take 44 hours to respond to generated leads. That's DAYS!

In fact, 77.17% of the leads that were submitted never received a phone call.

And the people making those delayed call attempts had a connection rate close to 0% on their first attempt.

In fact, this did not surprise me. I've interviewed a lot of potential clients for my own lead-generation services. I always ask how long it takes them on average to call their leads. A large percentage will say "as soon as possible." When I probed further, I found out "ASAP" often meant "a day or two later." They were usually lacking in other areas too, so often they weren't a good match, and I ended the call.

Where it gets more interesting is when you look at the response times after 5 minutes. There is a 4.5X improvement in connection rate from call attempts within 10 minutes to call attempts within 5 minutes. If you take longer than 5 minutes after a lead is generated to make a call attempt, you are only a small fraction as likely to reach them on the first call attempt.

And the response rate continues to plummet after 10 minutes. The odds of contacting a lead drop by 100 times if they are called after 30 minutes instead of 5 minutes!

An earlier 2007 MIT Study by Dr. James Oldroyd replicated similar results. They found contact rates dropping by 100 TIMES when leads were contacted after 30 minutes versus 5 minutes.

* * *

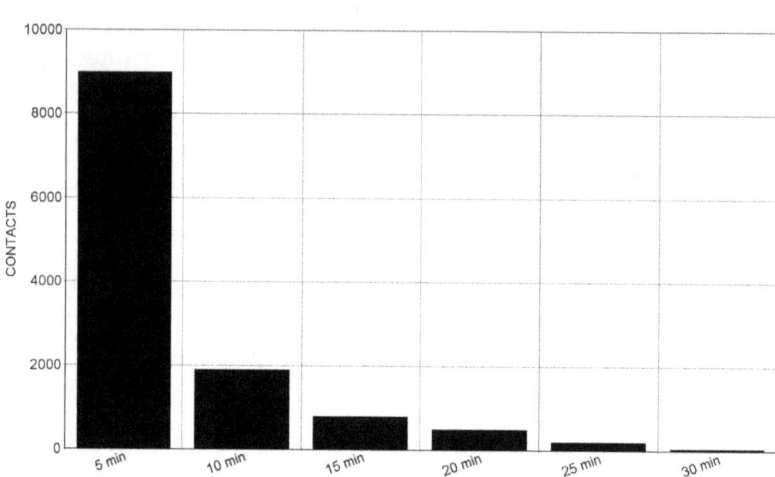

CONTACTS MADE FROM FIRST DIALS

Fig. 12. Contact Rate vs Lead Response Time for First Dials. Response Audit, 2016, InsideSales.com Harvard Business Review, Lead Response Management Best Practices

What does this illustrate?

It shows you should make every effort to ensure you're able to make call attempts within 1 minute of each generated lead. You can make exceptions when you're with another client, or are at home during your dedicated rest and relaxation time, or while sleeping. But otherwise, there should be zero excuses for not being able to call within 1 minute.

I know a realtor in her 60s in Edmonton, Alberta, who can only use the basic functions of her smartphone. Yet even she can make calls within 1 minute. Even if she's driving on the highway and gets a notification, she's able to pull over. Then she'll tap the text or email icon, glance at the lead's info, then tap their phone number to call them.

If she can do it, then you can do it too. No excuses.

I've found my own prospective clients who specified taking "under 5 minutes" to call leads were also strong in other areas. Areas like knowing their LTV and ideal target market, effective use of CRM, and more. These prospects were also in the Top 5% of their industry in terms of earnings. Some were even in the Top 1% with assistants working under them who were also trained in sub-1 minute response times.

Why is there such a big difference from 5 to 10 minutes? One of the reasons is the lead was recently in the process of learning about your business. So you're still fresh in their mind.

They might even be expecting your call.

That's why they're over four times more likely to pick up within 5 minutes. By 10 minutes, they're thinking about something else or doing something else. Half an hour later, it's out of their mind.

And of course the faster you can call, the more likely you'll convert. So if you can call within 1 minute, then all the better. Your prospects will be happier too.

In fact, this was later PROVEN in an even more extensive study done by the company Leads360.

They tracked the results of 3.5 million leads generated for more than 400 companies that spanned a variety of industries.

But instead of just tracking how many leads were actually connected with, they were able to go further and track actual CONVERSIONS. Even accurately tracking leads that took months to convert. They were able to do this with statistical accuracy by using a combination of sophisticated tracking software, and tracking over 200 times more leads than the InsideSales study.

With this, they were able to discover you can CONVERT 391% more leads if you call within 1 minute versus 3 minutes.

I must emphasize you are converting them, not just reaching them.

* * *

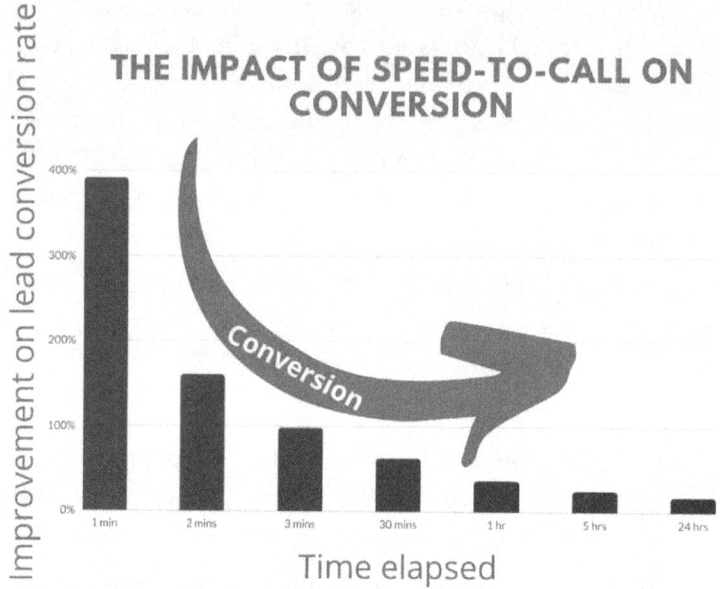

Fig. 13. The Impact of Speed-to-Call on Conversion. Leads360 study.

In fact, there is less of a difference in connecting with a lead between 1 and 3 minutes. But actually converting them skyrockets with just a 2 minute difference.

Why is that?

It's because it's so unique in a world averaging 44 hours of contact delay, that it ASTONISHES prospects when you contact them within a minute. It's so impactful, and they are so impressed, that they are almost 4 times more likely to convert.

You should want to astonish all your prospects. Not only to secure their business now, but to retain them for the long term. And have them refer people your way with the story of you calling them the minute they wanted help.

Here is a helpful way to enable you to call within 1 minute. Ensure your lead-generation sources are notifying you of new leads the second they are generated. Ideally, they're sending you email or SMS-text notifications.

Delay is the death of the sale, so ensure you are immediately notified. I immediately send both text and email notifications to my clients. It makes sense to help optimize their response rate.

But since seconds count, we can go further.

I like to teach my clients something I coined the "3-Tap" Method. It's where you practice contacting leads with the same way an Olympic athlete would practice their movement to further shave down the seconds.

It goes like this:

- Pretend you just got a lead notification on your phone. And take it out of your pocket as quickly as possible and turn it on.

- Tap #1 – Tap the app where you got the lead notification to open it (usually your text messaging app or email).

- Tap #2 – Tap your new lead notification to read it. (When practicing, just pretend to tap the lead, so you don't actually dial someone).

- Tap #3 – After reviewing your lead's specific info, tap their contact number to dial.

- Then while the phone's ringing, use those seconds to rapidly visualize a successful sale.

- Finally, keep practicing this (and ideally timing each run) until you are lightning-fast and can't shave off any additional seconds.

I can understand if this seems overboard for just making a simple phone call. But at the same time you need to ask yourself a question. A few moments ago, did you expect to learn that there is a 391% conversion difference between dialing at 60 seconds versus 180 seconds?

That's an over 3% boost in conversion rate PER SECOND. So just think of how much shaving down the seconds further could help your conversion rate. In fact, take a step back and ask yourself another question. Is there any other proven paid way to boost your conversions by a double digit percentage that beats just being at least a few seconds quicker? There probably isn't. And again, this is FREE.

Then just think of how such a conversion rate increase could compound over years of doing it. And then add on employees doing it too.

All with just 3-Taps.

There is one last way you can minimize connection delay to under 1 minute. Without going into details, it involves using a live chat integration on the website where prospects submit their information. That way they can be contacted without them even leaving the page.

Of course this requires you to hire multiple people to be ready for live chat. A number of the 48 studies I harvested mentioned this live chat advantage. Though they were focused on the B2B sphere where it was actually practical for medium or large-sized companies to utilize. But even if you aren't a medium-sized company in the B2B sphere, you can still get a close enough result. Just set up the right conditions to be able to call new leads within 1 minute. And the 3-Tap strategy will likely be a valuable part of that.

The HBR study also showed the best days of the week to make additional call attempts were Wednesday and Thursday. Additional call attempts were 49% more likely to connect on those days.

Now, this doesn't mean you should only make call attempts on those days. Still, make them as soon as possible. But it could be a good reason not to take Wednesday or Thursday off. At least be extra available to make additional call attempts on these days.

What happens if you don't reach them on the first call? Or even if you call within 1 minute, what happens if you don't reach them? Or what if a lead comes in when you're on your R&R time?

The next most significant findings from both studies were the optimal amount of additional call attempts you should make.

The first call attempt on average only has a 35% chance of making contact with a lead. As you make more and more call attempts, this average rate of contact can be raised to 90% by the sixth additional call attempt.

CHANCE OF MAKING CONTACT AFTER ADDITIONAL CALL ATTEMPTS

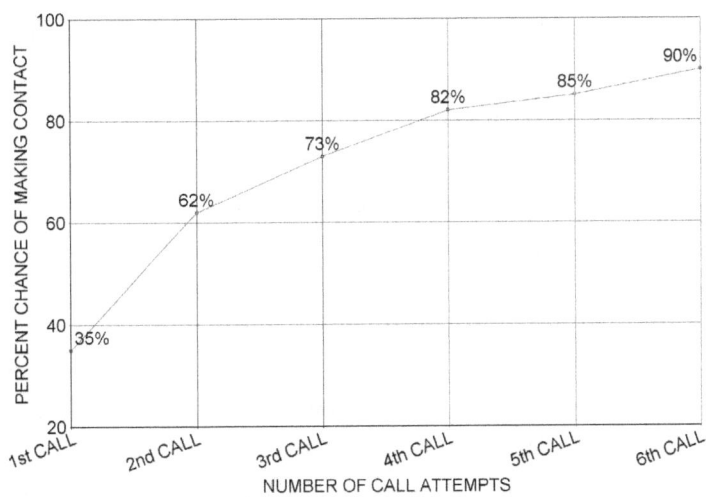

Fig. 14. Triple Your Connection Rate By Making At Least Six Call Attempts. Number of Call Attempts vs Chance of Making Contact. Response Audit, 2016, InsideSales.com Harvard Business Review, Lead Response Management Best Practices

This means you can almost TRIPLE your conversion rate by going from one call attempt to six call attempts. That's because you'll be connecting with three times as many leads. And these are leads you've already paid for. So you aren't paying a dime more for this boost. And shouldn't you want to get every last ounce of conversion from the prospects you've paid for?

So always make at least 6 call attempts per lead. One good way is to keep a list of unreached leads on a note on your phone or computer, and then dial through them when you make your additional attempts. Or ideally keep track of your number of call attempts via effective CRM software, which we'll discuss in the next chapter.

The Leads360 study goes further. While the HBR study found you reach around 90% of leads after six call attempts, the Leads360 study found you can CONVERT 93% of leads by the sixth call attempt. So again, there's a slight boost in conversion. But this time your persistence caused the impactful "WOW factor." And it's again rewarded with higher conversion rates (even if only slightly higher in this case).

When are the best times to make additional attempts?

According to the HBR study, they found making call attempts between 4 and 6 pm was the best time to call. Between 8 and 9 am was the second-best time to make call attempts. For instance, you are 164% more likely to connect with someone between 4 and 5 pm than you are when calling between 1 and 2 pm.

So try to schedule your additional call attempts within these periods. Know that the periods from 9 to 10 am, and 3 to 4 pm also have above-average connection rates.

I recommend leaving a voicemail only on the first call attempt. Let them know you'll keep trying to reach them later. That'll save time when you're dialing through your list of unreached leads.

Now here's a secret to minimizing the average number of call attempts required to connect. CALL LEADS WITHIN 1 MINUTE!

That's it.

I must hammer this point since it's so beneficial, yet not easy to make habitual. Remember: what is easy to do is also easy not to do. The sooner you call generated leads, the more likely you are to connect. Then you won't have to make as many additional call attempts later on.

One last note on additional call attempts. I've talked with several business people who imagine their leads will be annoyed with the additional call attempts. So both they and the sales teams working under them make few to no extra call attempts. And they only convert a fraction of the leads they're paying for.

Of course, they couldn't be further from the truth. As long as lead-generation providers are generating these leads in an upfront & honest way, it isn't a problem. By presenting leads with an attractive legitimate offer, the vast majority will be happy you've called. At worst they might have forgotten or lost interest in the offer, and will say "no thank-you."

Most leads will be happy you were dedicated enough to try and reach them. There are a million reasons why individual leads might take more call attempts than others. Maybe they were camping with no reception. Perhaps they lost their phone, it was a busy week, etc. Some will be grateful you persisted and were able to deliver them your offer. Often in spite of what was going on in their lives.

This is especially true with higher-ticket prospects. They have more respect for people that are more persistent in reaching them to help. You will impress them with your dedication.

The study also found the more 'touches' you make with each lead, the more likely they are to convert. Touches can be call attempts, emails, SMS-text messages, voicemails, FedEx, Snail mail, etc.

So if you make six call attempts, send one email and one text message, and leave one voicemail, that's nine touches. That is twice the average rate of 4.47 touches per lead they measured. This shows why it's valuable to use a lead-generation service that automatically sends leads email and SMS-text messages from you. It will help prime the leads and make them more receptive to your calls.

You might be excited to reap the benefits of making additional contact attempts, but still have one lingering question. What is the optimal sequence for making these contact attempts? I mean, is it once or twice a day, weekly, or something else?

Luckily Leads360 used its tons of data from its study to find the most optimal contact sequence on average. And like their other findings, this is optimal in terms of maximizing CONVERSIONS and not just reaching them.

It starts with 3 call attempts within the first 2 hours of generating the lead.

For example:

- Call attempt #1 within the first minute. Which was found to increase the average conversion rate by an additional 156%. ie. If the average conversion rate was 10% before doing this, then it'd be increased to 25.6% after doing it this way.

- Call attempt #2 within 30 to 60 minutes after the lead was generated. Which was found to increase the average conversion rate by an additional 58%.

- Call attempt #3 within 1 to 2 hours after the lead was generated. Which was found to increase the average conversion rate by an additional 25%.

If the lead comes in while you are busy or after hours, that's fine. Just make these attempts at the next available occasion, including the following morning.

Then it was found to be most profitable to make the next 3 call attempts on days 5, 14, and 15. These attempts added an additional conversion boost of 22%, 23%, and 9%, respectively.

I know this sequence seems odd, but remember this data was collected from over 3.5 million leads across multiple industries.

Just as interesting is what they found happened when they looked at best email practices from their findings.

The Leads360 study found leads that were sent email messages in between phone contact attempts had a 16% higher chance of being contacted by phone.

In fact, they generated an optimal email sequence to be used in conjunction with the optimal call attempt sequence.

The recommended email timing they found was sending:

- Email #1 immediately (or at least within 20 minutes) for a 49% higher average conversion rate.

- Email #2 on day 4 for an 85% higher average conversion rate.

- Email #3 on day 8 for a 52% higher average conversion rate.

- Email #4 on day 15 for a 37% higher average conversion rate.

- Email #5 on day 22 for a 44% higher average conversion rate.

When you follow the recommended email timing, they found you can achieve an average gain of 53% in conversion.

Here's a quick note on the sequences. Again, these are just the optimal sequences across a variety of industries. Are they the best possible contact sequences for your industry, and your market, and your specific business?

Probably not.

But at the same time, they are likely leagues ahead of what the average business in your industry is doing (remember the average reply time was 44 HOURS). So the best practice would be to at least faithfully try this sequence long enough until it's standard. Then you can start to experiment with variations. But only once you have powerful and accurate lead and conversion tracking tools in place (which we'll cover next chapter),

Perhaps you are making an offer where it is unlikely the prospect will be interested for more than a week or two. An example might be a realtor offering a free list of luxury homes in the area. Then you can test gradually shortening the sequence length to one week, and then stopping and going back up when the results get worse.

Or you might be in a higher-ticket industry with a longer sales cycle. ie. Software-As-A-Service (SAAS). You might want to test extending and even adding on to the sequence, perhaps as long as a month or more.

Either way, it's important to test to find your specific optimal practice. But at least after faithfully trying the current known best practices. And of course you can only do this if you have a reliable way to track your connection rate (and ideally conversion rate too) over time.

Now, you might be wondering how text messaging fits into all this.

Unfortunately, there hasn't been a large study of best practices for SMS text messaging. At least, not when it comes to optimal text sequences by themselves. And not optimal sequences integrated with call attempts, emails, and other contact vectors.

But we still have some valuable texting findings to keep in mind.

Here is a short list of the top five lessons learned:

- Lesson #1 – With text messaging, you have message open rates around 98% compared to emails 20%.

- Lesson #2 – 95% of texts from businesses are read within 3 minutes of being sent.

- Lesson #3 –75% of Millennials would rather text than talk on the phone.

- Lesson #4 – A Call To Action sent to a millennial via text is 40 TIMES more likely to be answered than via email. ie. Just asking them to click a link.

- Lesson #5 – Salespeople that leverage a triple touch (phone, email and another vector) have 28% higher lead-qualifying rates than those that use just phone and email.

So combine these lessons with your own testing to find the best way to integrate text messages into your own contact sequences. Experiment.

And here's a rapid-fire list of three lessons from the studies on Voicemail:

- Lesson #1 – Leaving a voicemail can increase your conversion rate by 4.8%.

- Lesson #2 – The optimal voicemail length is between 15 and 30 seconds. Every additional second after 30 seconds decreases results by 2%.

- Lesson #3 - After the first voicemail, your time is better invested in just repeat call attempts alone. So don't leave any more after the first call attempt.

Unfortunately, when it comes to Social Media vectors, there hasn't been much study on the matter outside of LinkedIn. That's because most of these studies were focused on the B2B (Business-to-Business) sphere, where LinkedIn is very important. Suffice to say, if you are in the B2B sphere, you should test incorporating LinkedIn contact attempts into your contact sequences.

As for other social media platforms, there isn't enough data when it comes to using them to try and help you reach your prospects. So

I'd advise doing little tests here and there to see if reaching out on social media helps. But only as long as it's not too time-consuming compared with the valuable call attempts and email sequences. (These are reliable and time-efficient ways of connecting with prospects).

Though when you actually generate leads through specific social media platforms, reply to any inquiries ASAP. Then transition them to the optimal platform to close them, whether that's your website with an order page, or a phone call.

I found one more valuable idea from these studies.

They concern the value of reaching and responding to your prospects BEFORE your competition. This especially applies online, where prospects might be checking out multiple businesses. They might be submitting their info to each.

A LeadConnect study found "78% of customers buy from the first responder." Thus you're more than twice as likely to convert a prospect if you contact them before your competition. An industry study by NAR (National Association of Realtors) supported these findings. They found 72% of prospective home-buyers would go with the first realtor to contact them. Again, the realtors who contacted them after the first realtor were less than half as likely to go with them than the first realtor.

Now how can you help ensure you're the first business to contact prospects? Two ways.

First, apply all the best practices from this chapter. This includes calling in under a minute and making a sequence of contact attempts. This is not only to reach them period, but also to reach them first before anyone else.

Second, you can also experiment with different offers that target prospects who are early in the buying cycle. Maybe they just started researching, and haven't contacted anyone yet.

A good example of an attractive offer to people in research mode might be a realtor offering a free list of homes in a specific price range. It would be more likely to get someone who's started thinking of buying a house. On the other hand, an offer like "find the current market value of your home" might attract people closer to the buying or selling stage. These are people who are more likely to have been contacted by a realtor, and thus harder to convert.

Here's one last helpful idea.

I know this all might seem like a big change. Early on some clients of mine expressed anxiety that they didn't want to take longer than 1 minute to call, even at 2 in the morning. I showed them they had nothing to worry about, and there was a simple way to make this entire process stress-free at all hours.

Like I did with them, I recommend setting up a 'Do Not Disturb' mode on your phone. Every phone has a version of this. Do an internet search if you need help finding out how to set up yours. This will allow you to mute any calls, texts, emails, and other notifications (except alarms) for whatever daily time range you specify.

So some might desire maximum rest time and set it to mute notifications from 5pm to 9am. While other more enterprising people might want to set it from 9pm to 7am.

Pick a range that works for you. And don't worry about emergency calls from family or friends. It usually allows exceptions for your contacts and whatever saved groups you specify.

The late and great copywriter Gene Schwartz liked to talk about how most of our inspiration doesn't come during our work. It happens during our play and relaxation time from our subconscious. That's another benefit to having a dedicated R&R time. Let your subconscious work and spring inspiration on you when you least expect it.

So what happens to the leads you can't reach within 1 minute during your Do Not Disturb time? It's simple. Make your call attempts the following morning. Remember you'll still reach 90% of them as long as you make at least six attempts.

I hope that helps take the stress off of this process. Everyone deserves some dedicated quality stress-free time to relax and ensure peak performance.

In fact, things can be made even easier when your lead provider or CRM or both provide ways to automatically text, email (and even voicemail) your prospects in the optimal sequence. That would leave sequenced call attempts as your only job... at least until you can hire someone to do those too. We'll cover those throughout the rest of the book.

And again, all of the above can work from any source of prospects, even referrals from another client or friend. In those instances, you might ask them to call first to get them to introduce you and what you're offering to this prospect. This will "warm" them up for your call. Then get them to call you immediately once done so you can make your own call immediately and get the benefits discussed in this chapter. Even better, try having the prospect conference-called. And let the referrer introduce you and explain your results, which will mean the contact delay will be zero.

So, did you find these studies valuable and enlightening?

Now let's put it all together into a simple daily plan that will let you consistently maximize the number of leads you reach. And this might only take less than 5 minutes per prospect if you're only leaving one voicemail, and have the emails automatically sent out. It'll require even less time if you're calling within 1 minute. That's because it will minimize the number of call attempts (and minutes of your time) it will take to reach them.

You have learned powerful best practices to maximize the number of leads you reach upfront. Even taking it to greater heights with Olympic-level training.

Next, after a quick detour to get some easy feel-good benefits, we'll discuss how you can nurture and convert more leads and past customers over time.

Exercise:

1. Make sure your lead sources are sending you leads the instant they are generated. Ideally using SMS-text and/or Email.

2. Set up the Do Not Disturb feature on your phone. Use a timeframe you're comfortable with. And don't forget to exclude important family & friends.

3. As long as you're not with a current client or on your Do Not Disturb time, you must call leads as soon as possible within 1 minute. Pull over to the side of the road if you're driving.

4. Practice the 3-Tap method until you can't get any faster.

5. Make a list on your CRM, phone note app, or paper pad (whatever you use) of the names and numbers of all your unreached leads.

6. Try to make your first three call attempts within the first two hours of generating a lead, or first thing the following morning if they come in after hours.

7. Then, while keeping track, try to mimic the optimal contact attempt sequence as described in this chapter. This includes phone and email.

8. Also test incorporating text messaging and maybe even LinkedIn messaging into your contact attempts, depending on your industry. Either way, it's worth testing.

9. When you reach a lead, whether it's a yes or a no, remove them from your connection-attempts list.

CHAPTER EIGHT

Free Generosity

"Wealth is not to feed our egos, but to feed the hungry and to help people help themselves."

- Andrew Carnegie

When you study how the wealthiest people invest their time, you might be surprised to learn a large focus of their time (and money) is on charity and helping people. Now of course there exist the comically stingy affluent with bowler hat and cigar, but they are in the minority, not the average. Wealthy people could spend their time doing almost anything. However, many find it most rewarding to help others via their time, money, and influence. I learned much of this from Dan Kennedy's book 'No B.S. Marketing to the Affluent.'

This shouldn't be a surprise, since many studies have been done on the benefits and satisfaction received from helping others. People who help others live longer and more fulfilling lives. And (as I'll touch on in a later chapter) people who donate more to charity, actually make more money.

I want to give you the opportunity to get these benefits during your experience with my book.

I have a question first.

Would you help someone like you, whom you've never met, if

you didn't get any credit for it?

And to make it extra compelling, would you help them if it was free to do so?

If you would, then I have a request to make on their behalf. And you might never get to meet them.

They are like you. Or at least like you were a short while ago.

New at all this.

Perhaps just a little jaded from the time they've been wasting on articles, podcasts, and YouTube videos from so-called "Gurus." And it led to very little actual improvement in their success.

Yet they're still hungry.

They want to succeed.

They're just unsure of where to look for valuable advice that leads to results.

This is where you can help...

The only way I can help small businesses succeed in getting more customers, is to actually reach them first. And most people judge a book on its reviews (and its cover too).

So would you please take a brief moment right now to quickly leave an honest review of this book? It won't cost you anything and will take less than a minute.

You're review will help...

...one more business owner support their family.

...one more entrepreneur make it in an industry they find meaningful.

...one more customer get more prompt immediate service and maximum value as a lifetime customer of a future reader of this book.

...one more life to succeed faster, succeed bigger, and succeed more easily than they otherwise would.

All you have to do is spend less than 60 seconds to leave a review.

If you are using audible: tap the 3 dots in the top right, tap rate &

review, then leave a couple sentences about the book with a star rating.

If you are using a kindle or eBook reader: scroll to the bottom of the book, then swipe up and you will automatically be asked for a review.

If the functionality has changed or for whatever reason you can't leave a review those ways: just go to the book's page on Amazon (or wherever you got the book) and leave a review on the page.

If you help a random person like that, then you're my kind of reader. And I'll be that much more enthused to help you in the following chapters (you'll love how I'll save you more time and help take the pain away at every possible step).

This is an idea I got from author Alex Hormozi. I'm glad people were generous enough to leave reviews to help those browsing his book. It's a great way to both get some easy feel-good benefits, while also actually helping many others out there who are just like you.

Also, if you got value out of this book, and know someone it can help, send it their way once you've finished it.

Thank you. Now back to multiplying your customers...

-Your fan,

Fraser

CHAPTER NINE

How To Easily Manage Your Customers And Communications

What's an easy way to manage and make customers more valuable?

Simple. Use a Customer Relationship Management service (CRM) to help manage and nurture your leads.

What is a CRM?

A CRM is a software tool. It's a database that holds all your past customers and prospective customers. You can upload them manually one at a time. Or you can upload a bulk list of customers if you have them in another digital format like an Excel spreadsheet. Sometimes you can even have new customers added automatically depending on which CRM you are using.

Then you can keep track and alerted of schedules you have set up for serving and nurturing each customer. This might be a combination of emails, calls, texts, letter mail, and any other ways you want to schedule contact. The CRM can even do some of these automatically, saving you even more time. So in the end what you're left with is a set of daily todos with certain parts of your database. This way you don't have to try and remember who you were planning on reaching out to.

Now a CRM isn't necessary for all business types, but a lot of companies can benefit from having one.

When you get a lead, you might manually enter them into your system. Or depending on your lead-provider and the specific CRM you use, each lead might be able to be automatically entered. This helps you better organize your prospects and customers.

It also organizes any notes you might have on them. It can show your history with them and your future schedule with them. Again, you can schedule reminders. This could be for things like future calls, packages, meetings, SMS texts, and especially emails.

CUSTOMER RELATIONSHIP MANAGEMENT

Fig. 15. CRM stands for Customer Relationship Management. Image Credit: Novasoftware

An entire sequence of emails can be set up to be automatically delivered over a set period. That could be over the first week, over months, or even over years. You can specify the time between emails to maximize the value you bring to them with your sequence, and thus the value you get back. So you can send your customers and prospects the most appropriate emails at the most appropriate time in your relationship.

This isn't something you can do automatically with just a basic email account. Especially not when you have hundreds of leads and past customers you want to send email sequences to.

This is a common feature of most email autoresponder services, and many CRMs have email auto-responding built-in. There are also many other valuable features available depending on your CRM.

When you email your leads regularly, you can keep yourself 'top of mind' with your customers. This is especially important for industries like real estate where it can take many months for a lead to buy a home. If you spend that time staying top of mind with valuable content, then you'll be more likely to be the person who converts them.

You can stay top of mind by sending them valuable newsletters, tips and tricks, and other helpful content. And of course, mixing in the occasional relevant offer.

A quick note on email. Make sure you're 100% compliant with CAN-SPAM email laws. This usually requires you to only email people that have given you their email address. You must also include your address and contact information in each email. And provide them a way to unsubscribe in each email. I recommend looking further into CAN-SPAM laws to be 100% compliant if you're planning on using email in the future.

Many CRM and email autoresponder services already do this automatically. That can make CAN-SPAM compliance easier. They can include features such as providing an unsubscribe link at the bottom of every email. And they can also list your business address at the bottom of every email. Make sure you set these up before sending out emails.

And again, I must stress this; you must only email people who've given you their email. ie. They submitted it on your online form they filled out. Perhaps it was on an online sales funnel your lead-generation provider set up. You are not legally allowed to buy or look up consumer email addresses and prospect them. That is unless they are other businesses, and you are soliciting them for B2B products or services (and this is legal in your area).

Ensure you read up on CAN-SPAM to be 100% compliant. Also read up on your local regulations on calling and local Do-Not-Call lists too. Some CRMs even have Do-Not-Call list integration if you want to avoid calling them.

Some CRMs and email services can help reduce spam by automatically unsubscribing anyone on your list who hasn't clicked on a link in an email in over 3 months. Email providers track what percentage of your emails are both opened and clicked. If people aren't opening or clicking then the email providers like Google and Yahoo will start to see your email messages more like spam. So your emails will be more likely to end up in the promotions tab or spam box if few people are opening or clicking them.

Help improve this by either manually unsubscribing those who haven't clicked in the past 3 months, or have your CRM automatically do this if it supports this feature.

Also emailing more often can actually help reduce spam complaints. If you only email your list occasionally, maybe less than once a month, then subscribers might forget who you are and that they signed up. Then they might just assume your email is spam. But when you email them regularly, at least once weekly, then they'll know who you are and be more likely to open the email and click any links you send them.

But what if you're worried your emails will be looked down on (or worse, unread) because you're not a professional writer?

Could you still write effective emails then? Perhaps invest dozens of hours into grammar and writing books? Or maybe just give up?

Don't worry, the answer is simple.

If you can talk, you can write.

This is the plain advice from email expert Matt Furey. He was famous for making hundreds of thousands of dollars in a single weekend from his email promotions. And believe me, the writing he used was not Shakespeare.

Instead, it was very conversational.

Again, if you can talk, you can write.

Which is to say, you should write emails like how you would talk to a friend. Imagine you're sitting down in a booth at a diner with a friend you haven't seen in a while. You are trying to help them with a problem they have that you're a pro at solving. What would you say to them? Figure that out, then write the email the same way.

This will make it more conversational, and thus more converting.

Most email split testing has also found that writing your marketing emails just like how you'd write to a friend is more effective than standard flashy corporate emails with weird colourful text and images everywhere. And which many people immediately close after opening.

Instead, it was found to be more effective to write basic plaintext emails with some links. Maybe not capitalizing every word in the title, no fancy banners, etc.

Now trends change quickly in the email world, so as always, test everything. Test images. Test the way your links look. Etc.

But one thing that doesn't change is the more personal your email appears, the more likely it'll be opened and read.

This reminds me of an example from the legendary copywriter, Gary Halbert. Gary had the view that people would sort and divide their mail into two piles. A-pile mail and B-pile mail. Everything in the A-pile would be mail that looked personal. It would later be read. And everything in the B-pile was obvious advertising. It would likely be just thrown straight in the trash.

So Gary's major idea was to make all your advertising mail look as personal as possible, so you have the best chance of getting it both opened and read.

He was pretty successful with this idea, since it led to the most mailed promotion in US history, and grew a billion dollar company.

And the same ideas apply to email.

Make the subject line look personal.

Make your sender name and address (and profile photo if using Google) look personal.

Make the contents of your email look personal.

It's hard to go wrong doing this. With this as your foundation, you can always test current email trends to see if that boosts response.

When it comes to what you should write in your emails, that topic could be covered in multiple books. But I'm going to simplify it down to two basic email content styles you can test.

You can either send them purely valuable emails, along with the occasional offer. When I say valuable, I mean write them emails full of advice that would be helpful for someone in your typical prospect's situation. Think of it like watching a TV show, where 23 minutes are the show, and only 7 minutes are dedicated to the commercials. Again, this is a very simplified version of what to do.

Or you could make all your emails valuable, and make an offer in all of them. This can be done by intelligently segueing the valuable part of the email to your call to action (CTA). This is usually done near the end of the email. And your CTA might be as simple as asking them to tap this link to your website to check something they might find valuable. This could be an offer, or even an article that links to an offer.

Hope this short segue into best email practices has made you more confident in harnessing it to the max for your business.

Now, back to CRMs.

So, with a prospect, as long as you keep yourself top of mind, they're more likely to do business with you either way. They'll also be more likely to happily refer you to their friends, family, and peers. A CRM is excellent at helping nurture and generate referrals.

And for some industries, like real estate, where it's very cutthroat, staying top of mind and well-liked is everything. In that industry, a CRM should be 100% mandatory.

I won't even work with a realtor without a CRM now.

I've made that mistake in the past, when I've worked with realtors who used recipe cards or sticky notes on their wall to keep track of their leads. And unsurprisingly these realtors were struggling and not very successful at all. Especially compared to their TOP5 peers in the same city who were using a CRM and of course calling within 5 minutes.

I found out these TOP5 realtors were profiting MULTIPLE TIMES MORE than their peers. And they had no other inherent advantages.

They used smart practices and took massive action.

To help you understand how big of a difference this can make. The average realtor sells only 2 to 3 homes a year. Though when you take out the top 5%, and look at the bottom 95%, the median is closer to only 1 to 2 homes a year.

Unless being a realtor is just a hobby, then those results are pitiful. They are doing their job only once a year. It's no surprise there's a turnover rate for realtors of 30% a year. And 80% of realtors don't even make it to their 5th anniversary.

Whereas when you look at the top 5% of realtors, you see a very different picture. They are often selling at least a home a month. That's almost ten times more than most realtors do.

And these TOP5 weren't born rich. They aren't supermodels. They aren't geniuses. Again, they research, apply, and test the best practices in their industry and spend their time with other TOP5 people who do likewise. In this case, the best practices involve fast lead-response time. And they involve using a CRM to stay top of mind and nurture prospects (and past clients for referrals).

As they ascend, some get so much business they will only see their prospects by appointment only. And they also use one or more assistants who are trained in these same best practices. Craig Proctor is a great example of this. While his peers were selling 1 to 2 homes a year, there were years where he sold over 500 homes.

500 TIMES MORE than most realtors.

That's the kind of difference you can achieve when you take massive action ascending to TOP5 and beyond.

I refuse to work with realtors who don't have a CRM, because I can tell they aren't going to work out unless they change their mindset, actions, and peer group.

Now I make exceptions for most other industries since a CRM isn't always required.

For example, a roofer or plumber wouldn't be required to have a CRM in order to do well. Though having one would still help them generate future business and referrals. When their past customers need their gutters cleaned or have a leaky pipe, they'll be more likely to call back the person staying top of mind with them. Or if their past customers know someone else who needs help.

In real estate, even a realtor with mediocre sales ability who uses a CRM can trounce the recipe-card realtor with better closing skills. That's even if the great salesperson makes a great first impression. Most people aren't ready to buy a home right away.

This gives the advantage to the realtor who uses a CRM, because they always keep themselves top of mind. And that's exactly where you want to be when they're ready to convert. You want to be right there in front of them, having recently provided them with valuable content or information.

If you're interested in improving your sales skills at all, which you should be no matter what business you're in. Then you might have heard about the greatest car salesman of all time, Joe Girard. You might have even read his book 'How to Sell Anything to Anybody.'

At his high point, Joe was selling more cars BY HIMSELF than 94% of the car DEALERSHIPS in America. He not only outsold entire dealerships, but the vast majority of them.

He sold cars to 13,000 different customers. That's more than 13,000 cars, because many of these customers were repeat customers. They would buy from Joe again and again throughout their lives.

So what was his secret?

Again, he wasn't born rich. He wasn't a supermodel. He didn't start with connections. He wasn't a super-genius.

His biggest secret to getting to this massive amount of success was simple. He would send a hand-written greeting card each month to each one of his former customers. That's it.

Now, this was much easier in the beginning when he didn't have many past customers. Before he hit 13,000 customers, he had some assistants to help him.

And by doing that, he kept himself top of mind. So when people needed a new car, who were they going to go to? A dealer who shrugged them off after they got paid? Or the friendly dealer who's been sending them cards every single month over years? Obviously the latter in most cases.

And this especially extended to who they were going to give referrals to as well.

Past customers were going to recommend Joe to their friends, family, and peers.

ie. "Joe's been in constant contact with us all these months. Oh, he's great. He cares. Not like all these other car salesman I never heard from again. Joe actually cares. I mean, he's been mailing me month after month after month. I highly recommend him."

That's why he got so many repeat customers. The customer doesn't have to be limited to one sale, no matter the industry.

Some of the greatest and most profitable money is money from past customers. That's because you've already paid to get them as a customer. Most advertising expenses are to get the customer in the door. When they are already your customer, it's much cheaper to keep them buying again and again. That's true even for major purchases, like a car or even a home.

That's why for realtors, some of the most successful ones keep in mind the average person keeps their home for about seven years. So if they've been staying in touch and top of mind over seven years, they'll be much more likely to help past customers buy their next home. Not to mention all the extra referrals they'll help generate over those seven years.

Joe Girard had so much business that people had to schedule appointments to be sold by him. This is actually a common sight you see in any industry, the higher up the success ladder you look.

I know a lot of business owners would love to run a by-appointment-only business. And there's no reason it can't work in your industry either, as long as you're generating enough daily demand.

I hope you can see how this all ties into the advantages of the CRM. You can replicate what Joe did, except much more easily and automated with a CRM.

You can keep yourself top of mind so when customers are ready to buy again, or to refer someone, they're thinking of you. You only have to automatically send them valuable content week after week, month after month. And this applies to prospects as well.

A CRM could be your ticket to replicating the success of the greatest car salesperson of all time.

At the very least, it beats covering your walls with sticky notes or using gravy-stained recipe cards to manage your leads and customers.

So which CRM might be right for you?

There are many good CRM options out there. Even the lesser ones are good enough as long as they're easy enough for you to set up and use consistently.

So I'd recommend taking a step back and learning which CRM the TOP5 in your industry most commonly use. You should already be seeking out nearby TOP5 people.

Ask the TOP5 people you meet up with which CRM they use and how they learned how to master it. What people did they talk to? What books/blogs/articles did they read? What YouTube videos and online courses did they watch? Did they hire a coach or consultant to help them set it up and learn the ropes? How often do they send content? And so on.

Some examples of popular CRMs are Salesforce, HubSpot, Pipedrive, Infusionsoft, and Zoho. There are many more. There are also CRMs oriented to particular industries such as real estate or medical. Most CRMs are pretty good. The best one for you is likely the CRM most people around you are using.

Beyond any specific features, the most important criteria to look for is a CRM that's easy to set up and easy to use consistently. And both of those criteria will be much easier when you have nearby peers and friends who are using the same CRM.

The essential quality of your CRM is it's easy to learn and use. So it helps if people in the same office, building, or nearby are using it as well. If it's easy to learn and use, then it will be easy to use

CONSISTENTLY, which is key.

Also, depending on your CRM's capabilities, try to use it to automatically keep track of the optimal contact-attempt sequence mentioned in the previous chapter. This includes phone and email, while also testing SMS-texting and LinkedIn messaging sequences of your own.

In fact, some CRMs can even do some of the emailing and texting for you automatically. Just make sure it keeps track so it doesn't automatically send a message to someone who's already responded.

Now you have a powerful system to help you track, nurture, and convert more leads and past customers over time.

Next, we'll discuss some tips on painlessly converting prospects at first contact... even over the phone.

Exercise:

1. Continue to reach out and connect with nearby TOP5 people.

2. Ask them which CRM they use.

3. Find out how they learned how to set it up and use it effectively. Ask them what books, articles, blogs, videos, courses, experts, etc., they used to learn it.

4. Get an idea of what kind of sequence they use. How often do they send content? What formats do they use (ie. Email, envelopes, gifts, print newsletters, SMS texts, calls, etc.)?

5. Set up your own CRM.

6. Use it consistently to stay top of mind with your leads and customers. Do this by sending them valuable content like newsletters, articles, video links, notes, etc. And mix in your occasional offers as well.

7. Incorporate your contact-attempt sequences and reminders into your CRM, depending on its capabilities.

CHAPTER TEN

Eliminate The Pain From Selling

How about some quick tips to help you sell more easily on the phone and in-person without pain?

As a warning, in addition to multiple selling-experts, I got many of these ideas from Jordan Belfort, the former "Wolf Of Wall Street."

Fortunately, Jordan has reformed himself. He now promotes ethical selling as effectively as possible. His training attempts to help people convert every potential prospect who's qualified and can afford your service.

If you've never had the opportunity to do sales before I can recommend a great book to help ease you into it. It's been coined the "salesperson's bible" in both spoken and written applications.

For those in the know, can you guess what book I'm talking about?

It's actually 'How to Win Friends and Influence People.'

Now some of you might be thinking "That book... isn't it like decades old? Wouldn't it all be outdated by now?"

Don't worry, I can understand the skepticism.

In fact, I was probably more resistant to reading it than anyone, since my parents actually tried to bribe me to read it. (That was the worst way to try and encourage it, since it destroyed all intrinsic motivation for me to read it, even though I would have benefited from it at the time.)

Yet to this day, it's one of the "most-read" books on the planet. Just go to Amazon.com. Then check out their cool feature where they use their Kindle tracking to see which books are not only being bought the most each week, but also which ones are read most each week. And for years, 'How to Win Friends and Influence People' has been consistently in the Top 10 Most-Read Non-Fiction books each week.

To make this statistic really hit home, many of the Top 10 spots for most-read Fiction books are usually taken up by Harry Potter books. So to spell it out, this book still has the reader passion of a non-fiction Harry Potter, even though it's many decades old.

That's how valuable it's still considered. And that also helps illustrate how relevant its ideas still are.

Just how are its ideas still relevant decades later?

It's because we don't change. Humanity is the same social creature it was tens of thousands of years ago. Selling ideas that work today, will also have worked back then. And they will still work for the next hundred years… at least until human genetic modification and brain chips… and maybe only then will this book drop out of the Top 10 most-read.

Luckily years after I was offered a bribe to read it, I finally got around to reading it. Boy was I impressed. It revealed social dynamics (and opportunities) that were in front of me the whole time.

I put it to use in the social world first to great success. I was now able to rapidly build and nurture powerful connections with other people. And very easily too, even though I wasn't naturally the most social person.

But when I first started my business, that's when it benefited me most. I was able to use these ideas of influence to make closing people not only more reliable, but feel more natural and easy.

And that's what I want most for those just starting with sales… to make it feel as natural and easy as possible. This is because there's usually a lot of anxiety before you finally jump in and realize it's not that scary.

So I want to help minimize that anxiety and make it as easy and effective as possible for you.

Now onward into the best practices for sales. These strategies apply equally well both on the phone and in person. But let's assume you'll be making most of your sales over the phone.

Fig. 16. Selling can happen in person, over the phone, or even online.

First of all, the second a prospect picks up the phone, you should sound enthusiastic, as sharp as a tack, and a force to be reckoned with. AKA: an expert.

Each prospect will judge you within the first four seconds of a phone call. If you don't sound like an expert who cares and can help, then they are less likely to convert.

Also it's been found that confidently and assertively asking the prospect for the order gets a yes at a rate of around 70%. While asking for the order non-assertively only succeeds about 30% of the time.

Next, sell ethically. Sell only to those who your product or service is a good fit. And sell only to those who can afford it. Ethical selling is the most profitable selling.

If you don't sell ethically, then you'll likely have to deal with multiple problems. These might include customer complaints, bad reviews, declined payments, credit card charge-backs (potentially killing your merchant account), investigations from government agencies, and other issues. That is not a very profitable way to sell.

This is a good reason why you'll want to qualify leads both before and during your call. The advertising and lead-generation sources you're using should be screening in only the type of customer you're looking for.

If you're selling to pregnant mothers, then you don't want elderly men seeing your ads. You don't want them clicking your ads, and wasting your advertising dollars, your time, and their time. So you'll want to ensure you're calling out your ideal customer in your advertising. And you'll want to be presenting them with an offer only they would be attracted to. This will help screen out many unqualified people.

The second layer of screening happens on the call. Depending on your industry, you might have a list of qualification questions you need to ask to screen out those who aren't a good fit for your service.

This is different for every business, so ask your TOP5 friends what type of prospects they try to screen in and screen out. And ask what qualification questions they use.

If you're brave, you can even 'play prospect' and call the most successful businesses of your type in your local state/province, or country. Then see what types of qualification questions they use. Get an idea of how they handle common objections you normally face from prospects.

Next, you should always be working toward a single objective. Find out if your prospect is qualified and a good fit. Then focus on getting their info, scheduling a meeting, etc.

You can let the prospect go on tangents without interrupting them. You should never interrupt them. But always steer the conversation back toward your goal once you get the chance.

You're not on the phone to chat. You're on the phone to help qualified prospects solve their problems using your business. So every single second of the call should be focused on getting them closer to converting.

Most prospects will say 'no' at some point during the call. Usually, only about 20% of your hottest prospects will say 'yes' and buy without resistance. And about 20% will say no regardless. That leaves about 60% of prospects who need a bit more convincing to turn their initial 'no' into a 'yes.'

You should expect this 'no' and relax. As long as you've qualified each prospect as being a good fit for your business, then the sale is far from over.

What they're really saying is they need more convincing. They might need to be more convinced about how your product or service is great and can help them. They might need convincing you are a qualified expert who cares and can help them. And they might need more convincing your company is trustworthy and great.

So if they keep saying no, then keep focusing on answering their objections. And make your product/service, yourself, and your company all look more trustworthy and effective. If you keep at it then eventually most of the qualified 'nos' will turn into a yes.

If you've read a few sales books before, you have likely heard of the idea that there are both logical and emotional ways to sell people. I like the framing that people buy with emotion, and justify their purchase with logic. But either way, you'll want to sell with both.

So paint them a picture of all the beneficial ways your product or service will improve their lives and they will want it on an emotional level. But also justify with logical proof elements like scientific studies, performance figures, competitive rankings, and other forms of proof. Also harness social proof like endorsements and reviews from regular people and especially well-respected people in your niche.

When it comes to leaving voicemail, I recommend leaving just one after your first call attempt. Try to keep it as short as possible. Ideally between 15 and 30 seconds if possible, as recommended from the response studies in my HBR chapter.

Stick to mentioning:

1.   Your name and business name.

2.   The offer you're calling about.

3.   A number to call you back at.

4.   Let them know you'll keep trying to reach them.

Leaving one voicemail helps make it easier when you're dialing through your list of unreached leads. It's much faster when you don't have to wait for their voicemail and leave a message.

This is assuming you're not using a CRM or lead-provider that automatically sends a voicemail to new leads. If that's the case, then you won't have to leave a voicemail for your first call attempt.

Grant Cardone thinks it's better to leave a voicemail after every call attempt. But I know the numbers show the results from more call attempts trump the results from always leaving a voicemail. And I want to make it as easy and friction-free as possible for you to turn additional daily call attempts into a habit.

Give yourself a month or two of practicing additional call attempts daily. Then, once it's habitual, you can give yourself the chance to test leaving voicemails after every attempt. Then you can decide whether the results outweigh the additional time investment.

If you want more ideas on how to improve your phone sales ability, I recommend picking up Jordan Belfort's book, 'The Way Of The Wolf.'

Another great book to check out on selling is Frank Bettger's book 'How I Raised Myself from Failure to Success in Selling.' It's one of the top books on salesmanship.

The book's key takeaway is to treat all sales as a numbers game. When you know a certain percentage of people will convert, then you should be happy to know the more prospects you sell to, the more people you'll convert. And when you do this consistently enough, you'll feel indifferent to the sale and be completely outcome-independent.

This is such an important point for many people that I must emphasize it again. The best way to overcome the fear of rejection in sales is just to keep doing it consistently until you don't feel it anymore. Regular consistent repetition and experience replaces any remaining fear with feelings of indifference and outcome-independence.

And as you keep selling more and more, it becomes like building a habit. First it gets easier after a few weeks, then it becomes unconscious and automatic after months of selling.

Frank gives the important example of the legendary baseball player Babe Ruth. The key to Babe's success was he treated baseball as a numbers game. This approach allowed him to feel complete indifference after each strikeout or home run. Since he KNEW with GOOD FAITH eventually the numbers game would win it for him.

And the numbers game is always on your side if you work with it. This should help you eliminate the pain of phone selling. It'll soon be as easy and natural as breathing.

Also, many successful people report that as you become more successful, rejections phase you less. This is independent from the indifference you build from regular and consistent selling. So know that long term, from using both strategies, the more you sell, and the more successful you become, the easier this all gets.

One last tip. If you're in a business where you have to make regular call attempts, especially to return calls or to leads that came in after hours, then make your calls the first thing you do in the morning. You can then make your Dream 100 calls after these calls, which we'll discuss more in a later chapter. Save emails for after your calls.

There are sometimes important things in emails, but rarely urgent. If they were urgent, they'd try calling or texting you. Calls and texts are usually higher on the urgency scale.

And on top of that, as referenced in the HBR study, the earlier you make your call attempts in the morning, the more likely you are to reach people. And thus you won't have to make as many attempts and will save time. So just save your morning email until after your morning call attempts.

You are now well on your way to becoming a master closer. You might find it most powerful to eliminate any pain or anxiety by just seeing it as a numbers game. This will be especially true after enough practice that you become indifferent either way. Just like Babe Ruth. And with that pain out of the way, you'll be able to focus on the end-goal of converting every prospect that's qualified and closable. You can apply and practice these ideas both in person and over the phone.

Next, you'll discover what makes your business better than your competition's, and how that's attractive to customers.

"When you don't ask, the answer is always no."

— Ted Nicholas

"The best salespeople are those who are rejected the most. They're the ones who can take any 'no' and use it as a prod to go onto the next 'yes.'"

— Anthony Robbins

"You miss 100% of the shots you don't take."

— Wayne Gretzky

Exercise:

1. Ask your TOP5 friends in your industry what qualification questions they use to screen out prospects who aren't a good fit for your business.

2. 'Play prospect' by calling the top businesses in your industry as the type of prospects you usually get. See what qualification questions they ask. See how they handle rebuttals. Then adjust your own phone calls from there.

3. Focus on closing only those prospects who are right for your service and can afford it. Politely end the call if they aren't qualified.

4. Always focus every second of the call on getting qualified prospects closer to converting.

5. For the first month or two, leave a voicemail only after the first call attempt (assuming you're not automatically sending a voicemail).

6. Treat this sales process as a numbers game to develop a feeling of indifference to the sale and outcome-independence.

CHAPTER ELEVEN

How To Position Yourself Most Attractively

What's a USP?

USP stands for "Unique Selling Proposition."

It represents what unique value your business offers that is better than what all other local businesses offer.

Knowing your USP and making it short and easy to tell people will make it easier to sell people on your business.

Why should someone buy from you rather than from any of your competitors?

Your answer and USP could be:

- A unique and in-demand service you offer that no one else offers.

- Speed of service.

- Speed of delivery.

- A great guarantee or return policy.

- Measured results that beat your competitor.

And so on.

Take a step back and look at every aspect and angle of your business. There must be one thing you do better than your competition.

Also, make sure it's SPECIFIC.

Most people don't have a clue what their USP is. When I ask prospects, most will give me generic garbage like "best service" or worse, "cheapest price." HOW is your service best? Specifically! When prospects hear overused claims like this, most will roll their eyes and reconsider doing business with you.

Fig. 17. An example of the most overused and unbelievable USP.

Fortunately, you are reading this chapter and will find a specific USP from your business.

Another thing you should do is keep digging down to find deeper and deeper benefits. Do this by:

1.   Writing out all the features (and supposed benefits) of your business' services and products.

2.   Keep digging down by converting them all into true benefits.

3.   Keep going and dig for benefits of benefits until you reach the benefit level for each that is most VALUABLE &

WANTED.

To clarify what I mean by benefits (and benefits of benefits), I'll use the example of Toyota's scientific system for solving problems: the Five Whys. It's one of many factors that led to Toyota's rise and increasing quality over decades.

When an employee at Toyota finds a problem, they know to ask themselves a series of five 'why's to be absolutely sure they get to the true root of the problem. They will first ask why the problem happened, then ask why that happened, then ask why that happened, then ask why that thing happened, and then ask why THAT happened. Usually by this fifth "why," they've dug deep enough to get through the superficial reasons why something happened and dig down to the true cause.

You can apply this same strategy to find the most powerful root benefits your business provides.

When you ask the five whys about each of your business' major services and products, the result might look something like this:

We get people X, because it fixes Y for them, because that makes them appear more impressive to other people, which makes them feel more esteemed by their friends and family, which reduces any anxiety about drifting away from them or losing them.

Now that you've figured out your major business benefits, I found the best USP template you can use them in. I learned it from copywriter John Carlton. It's:

"We help [X GROUP OF PEOPLE] do [THESE BENEFIT(s)] better than [COMPETITOR or COMMON WISDOM] even if [WORST SITUATION POSSIBLE]."

Brainstorm and try to fill in the details of your business situation until you find a combination that can't be improved. But try not to overcomplicate it. Simple is better for your USP.

Here's one I just brainstormed for my own company:

* * *

"We help small businesses reach and convert qualified prospects before their competitors can by using the most profitable online advertising strategies better than most general "brand"-focused ad agencies, even if they are in a tiny market with few prospects or a giant city with heavy competition."

You'll notice I did not trash talk my competition. And neither should you. You should instead position yourself AGAINST the competition, not OVER the competition.

When you trash them, you lose credibility. Instead, you should list positive reasons why you are in a unique position to benefit them.

You can't go wrong by not trashing your competition. That is my official recommendation to you.

Though to be thorough, I will let you in on the secret way to do it effectively, which will likely still not be as effective as just not doing it at all. You can always test both approaches to find out. Here's how it can be done:

It's bad to trash your competition when you're just spouting off a common attack. ie. A salesperson at a Ford dealer might wrongly say "Pshh! Chevy, I'd never buy one of them."

The problem is it's too common a response and thus it's not credible to prospects. Just like how the "best service" and "lowest prices" USP examples I mentioned earlier are not credible.

Instead, it's more effective to position yourself against them while backing up what you say with proof (ideally in the form of backhand compliments). ie. The same Ford salesperson would be better off saying something like "Yeah, they've been in the business a while. Many people have heard their name. But it's too bad they don't do A or B or C, since the combination of those I've found to have increased performance by X PERCENT." Or whatever examples supported by proof you can dig up.

Always be specific when attacking competitors. And try not to use trash talk that is typical in your industry without any weight, reasons, or proof to back it up. Back up all attacks with reasons why and proof.

And ideally don't make them look like attacks at all to help maximize credibility.

But again, you can't go wrong by not attacking, and instead just focusing on optimal positioning of your own company. Like how a lion might position itself upright on a cliff staring at a beautiful sunset while looking majestic and respected. This is instead of looking silly trying to squash the squeaking bugs all around it with its oversized paws.

When you find your USP, you should make it front and center whenever you're selling a prospect on your business. Most people want to know the specific advantages your business can bring them.

And you don't have to stick with this USP forever. Talk to your TOP5 friends to see what USPs they use. And look to the most profitable businesses in your industry for USP inspiration as well.

One last point is you should avoid making your USP based on price. Only about 10% of prospects will buy exclusively based on price. And they are usually the most headache-inducing customers you could get. Low prices also limit your ability to buy more customers outside of direct referrals and "hope."

Low prices are a race to the bottom. You should want to race to the top.

So you'll want to sell to the 90% of prospects who base their buying decision on overall VALUE provided rather than price. You'll want to sell them on your USP and beyond.

You now know how you're better than your competition. And you've condensed it down into a simple elevator pitch you can use to help you convert all future prospects. You will practice speaking this USP aloud until fully memorized.

In the next chapter, we'll go deeper into how high you should price your services.

Exercise:

1. Ask why people should buy from you instead of your local competition.

   - What unique aspect of your business is better than what all your local competition can offer?

2. Avoid making "cheapest prices" your USP. This actually repulses most prospects, since only 10% of people buy exclusively based on price. And those 10% are also usually the most headache-inducing customers.

3. Avoid trash talking your competition. Instead focus on your own positioning, ideally with proof to back it up.

4. Brainstorm ideas with the following USP template until you find one that can't be improved: "We help [X GROUP OF PEOPLE] do [THESE BENEFIT(s)] better than [COMPETITOR or COMMON WISDOM] even if [WORST SITUATION POSSIBLE]."

5. Practice reading this aloud as your elevator pitch until fully memorized and it's a part of you.

CHAPTER TWELVE

Your Optimal Pricing For Success

When it comes to pricing their products and services, most businesses greatly overestimate how many people buy exclusively based on price.

As I mentioned in the USP chapter, only 10% of people will buy exclusively based on price. And that's also usually the most headache-inducing 10% of customers.

In fact, sometimes you might feel like you'd actually pay money to keep these "people" away from your business. But we are actually going to do the opposite. Instead, we are going to get the price-sensitive headaches out of our lives, and actually PROFIT MORE while doing it.

Fig. 18. Optimal Pricing is important. Image credit: Wikimedia Commons by Videoplasty.com, CC-BY-SA 4.0

There may be a few who are still not convinced that not everyone buys on price. Perhaps it's their comfort zone holding this belief in place. I'll first encourage these people to go back and reapply the exercises in the comfort zone chapter. Then I will hammer this disempowering belief away completely with a few examples.

If everyone bought based on price alone:

- Everyone would be driving a Kia, the cheapest cars. Yet we see expensive cars from Mercedes, BMW, Lexus, and Tesla all over the place.

- Everyone would have the cheapest phones. Yet the majority of Americans (heck, even the vast majority of American teens) use iPhones.

- The only restaurant people would eat at is McDonalds. Yet people are eating at countless other restaurants.

- Everyone who wanted a watch would wear a cheap $5 digital watch. Yet there are ranges of people out there with watches costing hundreds, thousands, even MILLIONS of dollars.

- And so on.

That should remove any doubt from your minds that people aren't as price-focused as you might've thought.

One thing you should definitely not do is lower prices, aside from special sales.

When you lower your prices, you lower your customers' emotional investment since they didn't have to invest as much. You also lower your customers' perceived value of your business. That's because they see it as cheap and maybe shoddy, or merely just average like everyone else.

And if your customers aren't invested in their purchase from you, then they won't invest as much energy into it, and thus get less results from it.

But when you raise your prices, you naturally get the opposite effects.

Your customers are more invested. They have higher perceived value of your business. And they get better results since they are more invested.

What customers are really focused on is value.

People want good value for the money they pay. And they want more value when they pay more money for something.

Some good news is you can increase prices more than you might think. And you can still be perceived as a good deal compared to much higher-priced options.

There's a relevant study referenced in the book 'Predictably Irrational.' It found people were willing to pay 350% more for an item when the price was framed against higher-priced alternatives. The process of framing one price against another is called "price anchoring."

A good example of using price anchoring is in my own industry.

Businesses are always a little price hesitant when it comes to purchasing SEO services, which are naturally expensive. This is the case even though they still have good proven return on investment over the long run.

But when I let these businesses know there are other businesses out there paying more than $25,000 a month for SEO services, they see my pricing as more attractive. And when the pricing is more attractive, they are more open to increasing their perceived value of my service and its ROI. And I further increase this by mentioning other benefits like taking customers away from their competition.

There are multiple ways you can increase the perceived value of your services and products, such as:

- Pricing that is high enough to benefit from the perceived value, but at the same time is perceived as a good deal compared to much higher options.

- Including relevant bonuses with purchase.

- A generous refund policy.

- A powerful guarantee promising they'll be happy with their purchase, and ideally reversing all risk so they feel the purchase is risk-free.

- Urgency from something happening in your market like a product release date or upcoming policy.

- Urgency you create yourself like a limited-time sale.

- Scarcity in that what you sell is hard to get, maybe also because your services are already heavily booked.

- How they get what they purchased. ie. A wedding photographer would increase perceived value by delivering the digital photos on a reliable USB stick enclosed in an expensive-looking wooden box wrapped in a bow... instead of just emailing them.

- Making the solution seem easy with many of the hard parts of it already done for them.

Now you understand how important it is to increase your prices. So you are likely wondering how to figure out how much to increase them by. You will find out in three ways.

First, do some competitive analysis. Look at the top businesses in your niche. Start with your local area. Then expand your investigation to your state or province. Then investigate nationally and even internationally.

Find the best performers in the whole world. And look for both what prices they are charging and how they are able to justify those prices. Or more importantly, how their customers are able to justify in their minds paying those prices.

Also look at what the top performers are NOT doing with their pricing. A good example is the realtor who sold the most homes in a year, several years in a row. His name is Craig Proctor. Sometimes Craig sold over 500 homes a year.

But did Craig have to lower his commission rate to 1% like many self-proclaimed "1% realtors" to reach this volume? Not at all.

No offense to the 1% realtors, but it should be clear that you don't need to limit your pricing to win big. Instead, find ways to maximize your perceived value like Craig did.

I could write a whole book on this process, but that's the core process.

Now you've done your own analysis and have ideas for both pricing and ways to justify it and increase your business' perceived value. Next, bring this analysis to your TOP5 friends and pick their brains for even more ideas and refinement.

Their input should help you make a list of refined ideas for pricing and improving perceived value. Go through this list and circle all the ideas that could be implemented in your business, and circle the corresponding pricing.

Now maybe your area has a down economy compared with other

areas of your country, and local prices are suppressed. If so, then you can adjust your price increase accordingly. Or you can move.

Or if you're especially ambitious, you can just expand everywhere as you grow and franchise your business. If that's your particular vision, then it go for it.

Ideally you'd first put into practice your perceived value changes, and then increase prices. But sometimes that isn't even necessary. Just do it.

Take the plunge.

Then keep testing and tweaking prices as you test and tweak more changes to your business to increase your perceived value.

This takes us to the most important advantage of increasing your pricing.

With this pricing strategy, not only will you earn more per transaction, but you'll be able to invest more in both acquiring and nurturing your customers. And thus, you'll be able to truly leapfrog your competition and make maximum money. We'll cover this more fully in the LTV chapter.

In the next part, we'll be discussing the tools and ideas you can use to help leapfrog your competition and dominate your market.

Exercise:

1. As mentioned in the previous chapter, avoid making "cheapest prices" your USP. This actually repulses most prospects, since only 10% of people buy exclusively based on price. And those 10% are also usually the most headache-inducing customers. It also severely limits the number of customers you can get outside of direct referrals and "hope." We'll talk more about that in the chapter on LTV.

2. Look to the more profitable and higher-priced businesses in your industry. Do some competitive analysis. How do they justify their high prices? Talk to your TOP5 friends too for ideas to maybe price yourself higher.

    - Heck, look over your goals sheet. Could you even

reach many of your ambitious goals with bottom-of-the-barrel prices? Consequently, could you reach your goals sooner by modeling the pricing and practices of the most profitable businesses in your industry?

3. Also do some competitive analysis when it comes to how these top businesses increase their perceived value. Go over the list of ways I mentioned earlier to increase your perceived value. Then talk to your TOP5 friends. Find ways that you could implement in your own business, then take massive action and do it.

4. Then with maximum perceived value, you will be able to charge maximum pricing like the top businesses in your niche. Thus, you'll be able to afford to invest in more methods to get maximum customers and leapfrog your competition, which we'll discuss in the next part.

PART THREE

LEAPFROG YOUR COMPETITION

CHAPTER THIRTEEN

Manage Your Time For Maximum Money: Know Your Worth

You're now motivated.

You understand the importance of spending more time with TOP5 people.

You've got a plan to take massive action to reach your goals and get everything you want in life.

You know the lead-response tactics to multiply your connection and conversion rates.

You've learned which CRM system local TOP5 peers in your industry use, and you're taking steps to set up and use your own.

Now, are you ready to learn some strategies to help leapfrog your competition and vacuum out all the business from your local area?

First, what do I mean by leapfrog?

No one has an obligation to rise through the ranks gradually. Anyone at any time can choose to redirect their career and begin to operate at a higher level they're prepared for. If you have written down aspirational goals, then you must recognize the fastest way to them is not via fighting through your peers. It's faster to leapfrog over them.

The only catch is you must ensure your comfort zone is prepared to leapfrog to that higher level. As long as you're prepared, then there's no reason to wait patiently.

I got this idea from Robert Ringer. He was a commercial real estate broker who leapfrogged his business very effectively. He was one of the first brokers to own a private jet. Throughout the following chapters, we're going to discuss potential tools you can use to help leapfrog your competition and get maximum customers.

Right now, we'll look into ways to free up more time and then make it as profitable as possible.

Let's start with an easy, yet impactful change. A "Notifications Cleanse."

I'm referring to all the countless notifications from your phone, computer (and even smartwatch) that are interrupting your day. And worse, they are usually wrecking your "Flow State."

Books have been written on the subject, but I'll explain it quickly. Flow is a state where productivity or creativity just flows out of you seemingly without end.

This can be illustrated when a writer is able to easily write for hours on end with the words just pouring out.

Or a business owner just killing it and converting new prospects left and right. They're saying all the right things. They're anticipating objections before they're brought up. And they're making each customer happy with their purchase.

It can even apply to the more mundane yet required aspects of your job. ie. Filling out paperwork that only you can do. But at least you're in such a state where you can finish it all in one go. That will save you time for more profitable activities.

And it of course applies to activities beyond work as well. From being in the zone while playing a sport, to just relaxing with clarity at the beach, to even competitive video gaming.

So we absolutely want to maximize flow state for both work and play.

But flow has a natural predator... unscheduled interruptions. And the biggest modern source of these interruptions are notifications.

Some people get hundreds of notifications a day from their

devices.

And each notification will take you out of flow. This will make you take time to first refocus on your activity and then more time to ramp up back into flow state (if you can even get back).

So for some, flow state is a rare privilege.

We're going to change that by first doing a Notifications Audit.

Take out all your devices and go into the settings for each. Go into settings for Notifications and look at the list of apps that can all interrupt your day and flow.

If you want to maximize your productivity and flow for both work and play, you should turn off all notifications for things that don't DIRECTLY help you achieve your written goals and vision from the Karbo chapters.

For example, if your Karbo vision is to grow your business enough that you can afford to climb Everest, then only apps that directly help grow your business should have notifications enabled. And this would also include apps that directly help prepare you for climbing Everest. ie. An app that notifies you of daily breathing-control exercises. But that's it.

* * *

Fig. 19. Notifications Cleanse Audit. Image credit: Anna Nekrashevich

Do this audit.

Two exceptions are social media where you directly engage with and generate customers, and also social media that directly helps you reach your personal goals. An example of the latter might be staying up to date on a secret Facebook group of people who've actually climbed Everest.

And that's it for the notifications that don't help you directly realize your vision.

Now, the notifications you do want are from the apps you use to communicate with prospective and current customers. This might include apps such as your CRM, phone, SMS-text, email, and again Business social-media profiles.

One last thing to keep in mind is to turn on your devices' "Do Not Disturb" setting during your R&R schedule. This will importantly still let you receive notifications of calls and messages from your saved contacts. So you won't miss any emergency messages from family or friends. Just a heads up.

There.

Now you're fully cleansed.

Just listen… Can you hear that?

Silence.

No more beeping or buzzing.

Just you and your journey toward realizing your vision.

And with maximum flow to help accelerate your progress.

Now, let's dive into a secret and easy way to manage your time better by focusing on maximizing your income.

From a time-management perspective, you'll want to do everything you can to maximize the profitability of your time.

A great exercise to help you see this more clearly was something I learned from the legendary copywriter Gary Halbert.

Start by taking a piece of paper and drawing a big circle on it. Then in the circle, write down all the actions and tasks involved in your business. From reception, to marketing, to face-to-face selling, to executing the service, to stocking the shelves, to cleaning, etc.

Then circle the tasks that ONLY you can do.

* * *

Fig. 20. Time Management Optimization Circle.

For dentists, this might be exams and procedures (unless you have other dentists working at your practice).

For realtors, this might be in-person interviews, showings, and closings (at least until you get so much business, you'll need to hire people to help).

For chiropractors, this might be delivering the report of findings, doing adjustments, and any other procedures requiring your credentials.

And so on.

Then find other people to delegate all the non-circled tasks to.

One common concern is quality. Can these people do as good a job as you? The honest answer is probably not, but if they can do at least

80% as good a job as you, then you should delegate. And if not, then just keep looking until you find someone who can exceed that benchmark.

You can hire a cleaner.

You can hire a receptionist, secretary, or personal assistant.

You can hire someone to set up pointer signs and home staging.

You can hire an accounting business to do your bookkeeping and taxes.

You can hire someone to clean teeth.

You can hire someone to do x-rays.

And you can hire someone to do your marketing. Especially if you want to ensure it's profitable and doesn't get you banned on Facebook or Google for violating their stringent compliance guidelines.

When it comes to the TOP5 clients I've worked with or interviewed, they all get this. They want to be spending every second of their workday doing the most profitable task possible. And at their level, that mostly involves a packed day at their office. They'll have pre-set appointments with prospects and past customers.

They don't waste their time stocking shelves, mopping floors, or fiddling with Facebook retargeting campaigns (which I can assure you they are no expert in).

I see this across many industries.

"B-b-but Fraser, I LIKE stocking the shelves. I LIKE mowing my lawn. I LIKE making copies. I LIKE changing my oil. I LIKE spending all weekend learning how to fix my plumbing instead of hiring someone to fix it in one-tenth the time and at a lower cost per hour than I make at my work. I even LIKE scaling the tartar off my teeth with a dental kit for dogs that I ordered from eBay instead of paying a dentist. I also LIKE…"

Sure you do… But when you hang around with TOP5 people enough, who value their time tremendously for both work and play, such preferences will change.

Now, after talking with nearby TOP5 people, you probably have a good idea of what hourly income people at that level are earning in your industry. And also what they spend most of their time doing to reach that number.

So with that figure in mind, look at the tasks on your page that aren't circled. The tasks you could delegate to others. Ask yourself if the time spent doing each of those tasks yourself is more or less profitable than earning a TOP5 hourly rate. I can guarantee they're less profitable than doing the tasks only you can do (which are likely the same tasks the TOP5 focus on).

I bet doing everything yourself is far less profitable than delegating as many tasks away as possible. That includes marketing.

Notice I didn't have you compare your current average hourly income versus those tasks. That's because soon you'll be taking massive action with guidance from this book and your new TOP5 friends. So you'll be improving your income as you march toward becoming a TOP5 earner yourself. So start from that mindset and hourly rate.

Then once you get there, you can use your maxed income to spend your time doing much more satisfying things than home or office work that can be delegated.

Maybe a deep-tissue massage. Perhaps doing charity work. Maybe playing golf. Or perhaps buying the favorite currency of the wealthy: time. Perhaps more time spent with friends and loved ones, perhaps on vacation in an exotic locale.

Or heck, if you're a real go-getter, more time spent making maximum money.

The choice is yours once you focus on maximizing the profitability of your working hours.

There is one sympathetic, yet flawed reason some people want to be a "Do-It-Yourself"er and do certain things themselves. And that's because they might have been burned in the past by poor service.

I see this occasionally with prospective clients. Some want to get very hands-on and involved in my services, or even learn how to do it all.

Often this came from them paying for marketing services like SEO without doing their due diligence. Then months later and thousands of dollars wasted, they aren't even sure if they got a single extra customer. They don't know if they even got a single extra visitor to their website. That's often because the dummies they hired didn't track anything, in addition to being inept.

I sympathize with these people, but I know ultimately DIY is an unprofitable road to go down. So I help show them a better way.

First of all, I completely shut down all attempts to get hands-on with my end of the service. Just as a brain surgeon would refuse a patient's attempts to help saw open their skull. It's for their own good, and I also will not be allowed to be bothered with my work. I will do my job in peace and make my clients money.

Next, most of the DIY stuff they try is often outdated and lousy advice they find on free blogs.

If you want actual results, then solid marketing courses can cost a lot. A good course on something like Facebook or Google advertising usually starts around $5,000. And any single course often doesn't give every pertinent detail, so you'll want to buy and listen to dozens of hours of multiple courses to get a solid grasp.

Marketing conferences can cost anywhere from $5,000, to $15,000 to $30,000 or more. And there are even marketing mastermind groups with members that pay $100,000 a YEAR to meet up only 3 to 4 times a year with other like-minded people.

Free advice is by definition worthless, since it isn't acted upon. People who pay will pay attention.

If you made a deposit of $150,000 for a full-page ad in the New York Times, would you risk hiring someone from an online freelancing site to write the ad for $20? Or worse, would you browse some free marketing blogs and attempt to write the ad yourself?

Wouldn't you rather pay a professional copywriter whatever it would take to ensure you didn't lose $150,000? And perhaps even make a nice profit with it? I think so too.

And the same idea applies to advertising on Facebook and Google. Either way, you'll be giving thousands of dollars to Facebook or Google to advertise on their platforms. Just as you'd pay the New York Times to run ads in their newspaper.

It's your choice whether you want to hire someone to make that advertising investment profitable. Or risk burning up your cash for nothing by attempting to do it yourself, while wasting your valuable time doing it. I think most would rather save their time and make a profit.

Though there are still some people who are beyond help. I wish them luck.

For the remaining sane readers, I recommend doing the circle exercise right now. Then put together a plan of action for delegating all tasks that aren't making you maximum money.

This can also apply to your business social media, as we touched on in the notifications audit. You could potentially use Social Media Management (SMM) services to apply effective Content Marketing to your social media. And then combine that with the person who handles your business communications. If you don't have one yet, you should eventually hire or outsource communications to someone else. Then have that person reply to all comments and messages you get across your social media accounts.

That will then take 100% of social media out of your life. Then you can take a bigger sigh of relief, and just be laser-focused on the few tasks only you can do and bring in maximum income. We'll explore that more in the Social Media chapter.

You can also of course apply the circle exercise to your personal life too.

Here are some time-saving services you might not have known existed. You can test some of these now. Or you can at least look forward to testing them once you're successful enough that the arithmetic shows the time savings justify the extra expense. Here are the ideas:

- Hiring a maid or cleaner service to keep your home clean.

- Hiring a lawn care company to keep your yard trimmed and looking great.

- Hiring a laundry service to pick up, clean and press, and deliver your clothes (or you could use your maid to do this).

- Hiring a personal shopper to buy groceries and anything else you want.

- Hiring a food prepper to prepare your meals for you to cook later.

- Hiring a personal chef to cook daily or weekly with plenty of leftovers.

- Hiring a driver or buying a vehicle with self-driving capabilities (the latter is becoming more affordable every year).

- Hiring a personal assistant (PA) to manage your schedule, communications, and errands.

Some of these services (especially the driver, personal chef, and PA) might require a longer period to grow your income to the point where you can afford them. But others might be more affordable than you'd expect. Look into them (and ask your TOP5 friends what services they use).

You've cleared out and delegated away all the tasks that weren't making you maximum money or helping your vision. I can now mention one last time-related tip.

Most business owners spend all their time working "in" their business, when they'd be better off investing a bit of their time working "on" the business.

What I mean is spending time taking a step back and looking over your business. Looking for any wasteful practices you can eliminate. Looking for untapped opportunities you can exploit. Looking for bottlenecks that are reducing your maximum effectiveness. And applying many of the ideas you're likely to hear from your TOP5 friends.

An hour spent working on any one of these ideas might be more productive than multiple hours doing your regular business work.

So try and dedicate and block out time to work on your business. It could be an hour a week, or even an hour a day. Figure out what works best for your situation.

Time is such an important currency. When you take a step back and look at your goal vision for the future, you must understand that time is the ultimate bottleneck for that future. The more time you remove from news, social media, and tasks others could perform, the more time you can invest in this vision. Thus, the sooner you'll reach it. The choice is yours.

You've now eliminated distracting notifications. And you can see areas in your business and life that would be more profitable to delegate to others. So you can use your time most profitably and most enjoyably.

Next, we'll quickly go over some online fundamentals that must be in place to enable you to leapfrog your competition.

Exercise:

1. Do a Notifications Audit.

2. Find your own 'story of Milos' to help anchor your commitment to only caring about things you can directly control and directly impact your future vision. This includes eliminating news and non-business social media from your life.

   - You can still get important industry-related news updates using Google Alerts.

   - You can even get business social media out of your life from a combination of hiring a Social Media Manager (which we'll cover in a later chapter), and enlisting your communications person to respond to comments and messages.

3. Take a piece of paper.

4. Draw a big circle on it.

5. Write all the different tasks your job requires.

6. Circle the tasks only you can do. You might find these tasks similar to what local TOP5 people focus their time on.

7. Find people to delegate the other tasks to.

8. Enjoy spending your time only doing tasks that generate maximum income.

9. Try to allocate at least an hour a week to working "on" your business.

CHAPTER FOURTEEN

Online Fundamentals That Must Be In Place

If you want to expand your online presence so people can find your business more easily and become customers, then this chapter is for you. I will cover some easy ways for you to get your business accelerating online and put yourself out there. And most of them are free.

If you are missing one or more of these (or if they're not as well-optimized as they could be), then this chapter will help you remove some of the biggest bottlenecks to your business. And you might not have been aware they existed.

You or someone helping you could set up most of these in an hour or two altogether. And they will act as great sources of future business calls.

Though depending on what marketing services you are using, a lot of them will include the price for the setup of some of these with services that require them. If you want these done on their own, then you can have someone professional set them up for you as well for a decent price.

My first big recommendation is setting up Google My Business (which I'll refer to as GMB). This is a way for your business to show up on Google search results when people search for businesses like yours.

* * *

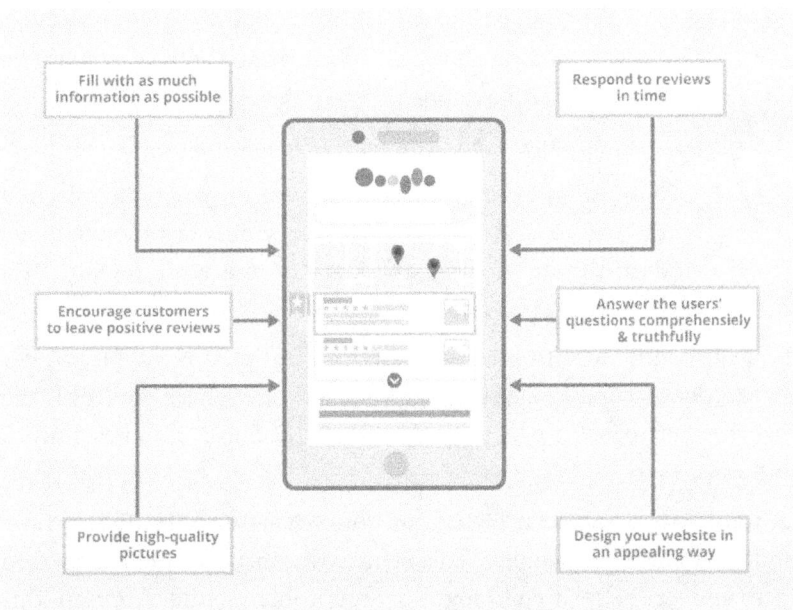

Fig. 21. Google My Business tips. Image credit: Seobility

Just search for "Google My Business" and you'll be directed to the simple setup steps.

Here are some GMB tips:

- Make sure your physical address, phone number, and email are correct. This is important for reasons we'll discuss next chapter.

- Apply for verification. When you do this, Google will mail you a postcard with a verification number on it to verify you are at this address. Make sure everyone at home knows to expect it in the mail and not throw it away.

- Ensure every single possible detail is filled out, and double-check to see that the public hasn't filled out anything for you that you need to correct.

- Make a relevant post once a week (set a reminder on your phone to help ensure this). People browsing Google will be able to see these posts, and they will take up valuable space that your competitors would otherwise take up.

- Use the Booking button to integrate with your online calendar (if you have one).

- Answer any questions you receive from prospects.

- Add any Photos and videos you have of: you, your place of work, before and afters, customer video testimonials, etc. And add more pictures or videos once a week (again, set a reminder on your phone).

Next, you'll want to set up a Facebook business page. Head over to facebook.com/business/pages/set-up . Then follow the instructions to set up a page for your business. It takes only 5 minutes.

You'll want to add a picture of yourself as your profile picture, and not your business logo. This is because lots of testing has proved faces convert better than a logos as the profile picture. After all, this is Facebook not Logobook. Though still put your logo in the cover image next to your profile picture.

If you don't have a good profile picture of your face, there are lot s of photo services in every city that could get you a professional-looking picture. This will help your conversion rate. It might only cost $10. Even Walmart provides this service.

Put your logo on both your Google business profile and Facebook business page's cover image (again, not the profile photo).

Then set a weekly reminder on your phone to post regular picture posts of your work. This could be problems you've found, any attractive projects you completed, before & afters, customer video testimonials, etc. Also remind yourself at work to take pictures. Ideally at least once a week should be good. This will help show people you're an active business too.

You're now prepared with a professional GMB profile, and Facebook page. Now we can start harnessing these in coming chapters to help generate customers.

Next, we'll discuss a service to acquire customers very profitably using Facebook and Google. And what traits you should be looking for in providers of this service.

Exercise:

1. Set up a GMB profile for your business.

2. Set up a Facebook page for your business.

3. And most importantly, get help or hire a professional to do any part of the above steps you aren't 100% comfortable with.

CHAPTER FIFTEEN

Get More Customers Today

Are you ready to learn how to get even more customers?

And are you ready to learn about the most cutting-edge customer sources?

Not a lot of people are aware of this, but some ways to source customers can take longer than others to convert, yet are still very profitable. Sometimes more profitable than customers you are buying now.

One of the best ways to get customers now is lead generation, which I will refer to as leadgen. It can be very profitable when it generates customers by advertising on online platforms like Facebook and Google.

It's one of the best ways to generate leads and convert them.

* * *

Fig. 22. An Example Lead Generation Funnel.

With Google, you're getting hot prospects who've SEARCHED for something related to the service you provide. This makes them likely prospects to convert.

With Facebook, you're getting hot prospects who are similar to past customers who've bought from you before.

You get customers from Google by what they're looking for right now. And you get customers from Facebook based on their interests and demographics; who they are.

Now whether you'll want to use ads on Google, Facebook, or both depends on what industry you're in.

If you're a plumber who wants a lot of emergency calls, then it's harder to make Facebook profitable. That's because there's no checkbox for "will have a plumbing emergency." But Google could be very profitable since you can specify to only show your ads to people searching for "plumber" in your local "city." Those are much hotter (and more profitable) prospects.

On the other hand, if you're a chiropractor looking for patients, then Google might not be the best place to source them. A lot of people with pain aren't yet at the point where they're searching for solutions. Facebook might be a better source of leads for chiropractors. That's because you can target the demographics of your most likely customers. Then you could advertise the various treatment options to them.

Though you must be vigilant to ensure you stay compliant with Facebook's (and Google's) guidelines. Otherwise, even using the word "pain" in your ads is liable to get your ads, or worse, your whole advertising account, banned.

In fact, Facebook is banning more and more accounts over time. And the rules and guidelines (even the ones we know of) are becoming less and less clear.

Fig. 23. A list of some of Facebook's guidelines that could lead to ad disapproval or account deactivation.

I actually got one of my own Facebook ad accounts banned just for logging on from a computer I rarely log on from (even though it wasn't a problem before). Their algorithms merely suspected something was wrong and didn't want to take a chance. Luckily I'm one of the advertising agencies with a personal dedicated Facebook rep, so she was able to help me get my account reinstated. I can't promise you'd get your own ad account reinstated if it happened to you.

That's one of the many reasons I highly recommend hiring a dedicated lead-generator instead of messing around with doing it yourself.

I provide leadgen services, so I can help guide you in exactly what to look for when browsing the different leadgen options.

It's different for every industry, but you'll most likely want the following six features:

1.   Leads that aren't shared with other businesses and bombarded with calls. I care about the leads themselves, and I'd rather have them happy than annoyed. Wouldn't you rather have happy leads too?

2.   Email or SMS-text notifications sent to you the instant a lead is generated to help you call within 1-minute.

3.   Very important: Qualified leads from a good offer that attracts good prospects. They are generating them from attractive offers your business can provide. ie. A list of homes in the area offer for a realtor, a discount gym membership offer for a gym owner, a contest with big prizes offer for a medispa, etc.

      -   What you DON'T want are leadgen providers that use inappropriate or spammy offers. Ones that ultimately generate garbage leads who are upset their time was wasted. They are likely no better than randomly calling numbers from the phone book (and maybe that's where they got their leads from).

      -   Use an offer that both attracts your ideal customer, and you can DELIVER on. So when they pick up the phone (less than 1-minute after submitting their info), they're happily expecting to talk to you. They aren't surprised, asking "Who is this? How did you get my number?" They're saying "Wow! Thanks for calling so quickly."

- Usually when prospective clients say to me "I got 300 leads from my last provider, and not a single one converted," I dig deeper and find out it was because their providers were using bad and inappropriate offers.

4. Leads are sent to a custom landing page instead of just to your website. No matter how pretty your website looks, nor how ugly you think the landing page looks, the fact is your website is usually optimized for browsing, while landing pages are optimized for conversion. Ie. People sent to a website might only convert at 1%, while landing page visitors might convert at 10 to 25% or even higher depending on the offer.

5. Email and SMS-text autoresponders to automatically contact the lead right after they submit their information. This will make leads better 'primed' for your call from these multiple extra 'touches.' It could be something as simple as an SMS-text asking when the best time to call would be to discuss the offer.

6. Reasonable expectations. This is big. You don't want to work with providers who grossly exaggerate what they can do for you. You don't want to hear them claim "every single lead is hot, and you'll convert 80% of them." You'll want to work with ones who are honest. Ones who'll admit:

- There will be a range of lead quality. There will usually be a small percentage of fake numbers/ emails. There will be a big percentage of leads who leave their real contact info, but won't reply to the first text or email sent by the autoresponder. And then there will be a big percentage of leads who will give accurate info AND reply to the text or email autoresponder message, sometimes before you can even call them. This latter category represents the hottest type of lead.

- For most industries, the lead conversion rate will be between 10% and 30%. Sometimes higher and sometimes lower. Though the conversion rate on its own isn't everything. What matters is overall profitability. This includes conversion rate, average cost per lead, and average number of leads per month. With those numbers you can calculate exactly how profitable the program can be.

All these features should be mandatory in any leadgen provider you are considering.

A lot of my clients find the email and text autoresponders especially valuable. When their leads are automatically sent an email and SMS-text right after they submit their info, this not only helps prime them for their call, but it has an added benefit.

Many clients aren't used to calling prospects who aren't referrals from friends, family, or past customers. So they aren't used to the lower conversion rates and more frequent "no thank-you"s. While they might convert up to 80% of direct referrals, they might only convert 20 to 30% of leadgen-sourced leads. For niches like realtors, it could be even lower.

Those are still very profitable percentages, but I can understand why it can be a little intimidating. Unfortunately, some clients find this so intimidating they won't even call at all. Often making excuses and delaying until it's too late.

It happens more often than you think.

Part of it might be their 'comfort zone' trying to push them back to only dealing with direct referrals. Though they could profit so much more with leadgen. But they don't call, they complain the leads didn't work, and then go back to what they were doing before. I know for a fact they didn't call, because I called the leads myself to figure out what was wrong.

I also started to use this threat of me calling the leads with new clients. This was to help get them into gear and help turn not calling and "the leads aren't working" into calling and "this is great."

But even then, I still wanted to find a way to help make it easier for clients to get used to calling their leads without having to threaten to call them myself.

And this equally applies to and benefits clients who aren't used to the sheer volume of leads I send. They might find it intimidating.

So I found a solution that greatly increased their calling confidence. I made sure all the leads were sent email and SMS-text autoresponder messages right after they're generated. I usually like to use a message asking when would be a good time to call to discuss the offer. This not only helps prime the leads for the call. It also got about 30 to 60% of the leads to respond back.

Some of the responses would even come almost immediately, in under 5 minutes before my clients could call. This helped put my clients at ease and made them feel better about reaching out to these non-referral leads.

My clients liked seeing reply texts like "call me now" or "I'm in meeting. Call at 2:30" or "call tomorrow morning," etc.

So even if you aren't able to reach them during the first attempt, then at least a percentage of leads will let you know the best possible time for an additional call attempt.

This is especially important with millennials. A study found 60% of millennials will text back after ignoring a call.

When I first applied this technique with a roofing client, I turned complaints about my leads (that I found out were never called) into praise for this new method. She was now happy to call all these people who were texting her good times to call. And then she got happy enough to call within 5 minutes whether they replied or not.

I knew from then on I must use this autoresponder technique with every client.

Funnily enough, some of these leads will reply with several paragraphs via SMS-text messages. Usually to my realtor clients letting them know exactly what they're looking for and for what price range. That's another BIG advantage of this method. It helps you better identify HOTTER leads who are more likely to convert.

The leads who reply quickly, reply with specifics, write long replies, and reply period are some of the hottest leads you can find. You can use this info to help segment them for more time investment from you since they're more likely to convert.

This process can also sometimes incorporate automatically sent voicemails. Though that usually only helps conversion rate up to 6%, and only for certain industries.

Some businesses would also benefit from having an entire sequence of messages sent to their prospect until they respond. ie. Sending them a sequence of a combination of 9 emails and text messages over 7 days, or until the prospect is ready to respond. So the messaging stops automatically as soon as they call, email, or text reply.

The big advantage of this is you wouldn't have to contact any lead until AFTER they've responded. Some people just lead hectic lives, so the appearance of persistence on your part will be rewarded.

This doesn't work for businesses that utilize online calendars to take bookings. That's because it's sometimes difficult to connect the various software services to stop the automatic messaging.

On the other hand, if you are a business that can benefit from taking bookings from online calendars, then I highly recommend utilizing them. They can even be linked in the initial automatic text and email messages to each lead. So the lead has a chance to book an appointment with you before you even reach out yourself. This is great for a variety of businesses like salons, wedding photographers, etc.

One trap some businesses get into is they try to get overly targeted. They might specify they only want households making over $200,000 or live within a 4-minute drive from their business. They try to force this criteria on their lead provider because they think this will help them get the best conversion rate possible. Maybe they heard a peer mention this idea. Who knows?

The problem with that is it not only doesn't guarantee a higher conversion rate. But it also puts too much importance on conversion rate in the first place. Conversion rate is just one of multiple factors. A good lead-generator will instead try to optimize OVERALL PROFIT for their client. Money in the bank.

This involves carefully optimizing not only conversion rate, but also cost per lead, and the number of leads per month. Only when you optimize for all three together are you able to achieve maximum profit. This is another reason I don't let clients get "hands on" with my marketing.

You now know how powerful leadgen can be to profitably generate customers. And you know what to look for in providers.

Next, we'll discuss a longer way to get customers, but even more profitably.

Exercise:

1.   Look for a lead generator with these benefits:

- No shared leads. Each lead is sent only to your business.

- Leads shall be sent immediately after they're generated via SMS-text or email, or directly to your CRM.

- Use an offer that attracts only qualified leads who are happily expecting your call.

- Email and SMS-text autoresponders to help contact and prime the lead for your call. If possible, use autoresponders that can deliver an automated sequence of messaging until the prospect is ready to respond (ie. 9 messages over 7 days).

- Reasonable expectations.

CHAPTER SIXTEEN

Get More Customers In The Future

Getting customers today is always desirable. But what if there was a method that got you customers in the future, yet even more profitably than more immediate methods?

That brings us to using Local SEO as a marketing source of leads.

Fig. 24. Oversimplified diagram of Google's Page-rank algorithm. What SEO is based around. Image Credit: Wikimedia Commons by

Felipe Micaroni Lalli

SEO stands for "Search Engine Optimization." It's a common marketing service many companies use to generate leads, both successfully and unsuccessfully. I know some people get burned because they don't do their due diligence. They later find out their SEO provider didn't have a clue.

That turns many people off of digital marketing period when they've had bad experiences with SEO providers and "gurus." But know not all SEO providers are like that.

While we're talking about it, what is SEO?

Basically, you're paying people to optimize your website and generate content and links for it. This makes your website look more attractive to Google, so Google will rank your website higher on its search results.

And the higher your site is ranked on Google, the more people you'll get clicking the link to your website instead of a lower-ranked competitor's website.

The company Advanced Web Ranking collected data on the distribution of clicks among the different search results. What they found was interesting.

They found 75% of all clicks will go to the websites on the first page of search results. 33% of clicks will go to the top search result, with 15% going to the 2nd result, and 9% going to the 3rd result.

This illustrates how valuable SEO can be to help you get ranked as high as possible.

The problem is these results aren't instant. Even with the best SEO provider, it can sometimes take from 6 to 12 months or more to raise your search result position to where you want it. It's rare for it to work in the first month or two.

This leads to other potential problems.

The first one is impatience. Some people don't want to wait months for SEO to become profitable, even if it will deliver a higher return on investment than their current results. They can only see a month ahead and want customers this month. They do not have the patience to let themselves make maximum money.

This impatience can backfire even further. They might then start believing particular SEO provider claims that they can get them to the top of Google in a month or two. They claim this for either two reasons. They could either be lying or just incompetent, and will ultimately fail to make much of an impact at all.

Or worse, they could be telling the truth and using dangerous "blackhat" methods. They will try and trick Google into ranking them very quickly with fake website links. While this might work for a few months, know Google will likely not only find out and crush you back down, wasting all your SEO consulting dollars. But they could go further and even blacklist your site so few will ever see it again.

You could lose many potential profits by working with the wrong SEO provider.

Now in certain fad niches this might be a good strategy. But for 99% of normal businesses, you should only look for honest and legitimate "whitehat" SEO providers. That's if you want your site to be visible on Google for longer than a few months.

You should also be looking for an SEO provider that provides monthly reports, so you're not left in the dark with what's going on. And one that gives a reasonable timeframe for results.

The only typical problem with traditional SEO services is the cost. There are some companies spending over $25,000 a month on SEO. And most businesses can expect to spend at least into the thousands of dollars to be able to outrank the competition for the number one position (especially if you're in a big city with many other competitors putting thousands a month into their own SEO efforts).

But luckily there's a relatively new alternative. It's called Local SEO, and it doesn't require as much of a monthly investment as traditional SEO.

So what is Local SEO?

Remember your GMB profile I had you set up in a previous

chapter? Well, Local SEO is all about making your GMB profile rank above other businesses' GMB profiles when people make a Google search. And your profile will direct prospects to you via your phone, website link, and business address on the map.

Because most of the money going into SEO is going into traditional SEO, and less is going into Local SEO, that makes it require less of a monthly investment to rise above your local GMB competition.

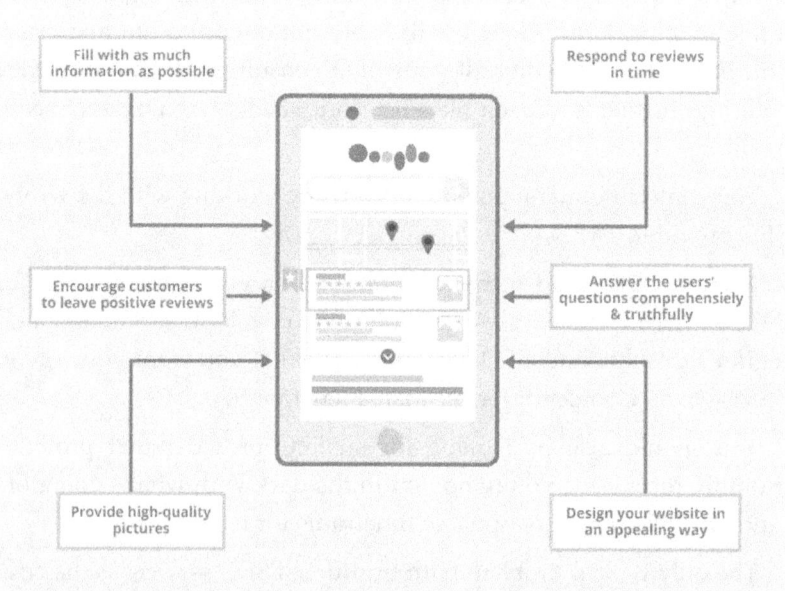

Fig. 25. Local SEO helps you rank your Google My Business listing above your competition. Image credit: Seobility

Now, I'm not saying traditional SEO is over. It's still quite profitable. But when you're just getting started with SEO, it's a good idea to start with Local SEO and rank your GMB first and get more customers that way. Then you can later use the surplus income from your Local SEO rankings to later fund traditional SEO attempts to raise your website rankings (and income) too.

Or if you have a lot of surplus income already, you can get started on both so that you'll have the number one position that much sooner.

The choice is yours.

One interesting advantage of getting both types of SEO is that you'll gradually be able to make more and more of the first page of Google search results contain digital real estate from your business. From your GMB to your website links. And this can even include other properties like SEO-optimized YouTube videos that show up. The important idea is the more real estate you have on that first page, the more likely a prospect will click through to you instead of a competitor.

I thought about putting some SEO tips you could do yourself into this chapter, but that wouldn't be fair to you. Tips like doing keyword research, optimizing your keyword density, image alt-tags, and other variables to tweak alone might have enabled you to reach the top position a decade ago. But nowadays you need much more to even have a chance at competing by yourself. I'm talking hundreds of dollars a month just for the research tools alone like Semrush and Ahrefs. Then thousands of dollars for SEO courses and subscriptions to current best practices. And that's before we get into link-building, which might cost into the hundreds of dollars for a single link... That is if you want a link with high enough trust value that you won't risk Google penalizing you and potentially blacklisting your site. And so on.

So if you want to do it yourself for whatever reason, that's what must be done. But as in my time management chapter, I heavily recommend just hiring a white-hat Local SEO provider and let them do it properly and safely and effectively.

Ranking higher on Google search results via SEO is often the most cost-effective source of leads outside of referrals from past customers.

It can just take a while to kick into gear. So when you can accept that timeframe, you can profit considerably.

Now since SEO usually is more cost-effective than leadgen once it gets into gear, does that mean you should drop leadgen at that point? Not if you want to make maximum money. While SEO is usually more cost-effective, it also usually targets different prospects from leadgen. SEO only attracts prospects from organic search. That still leaves many profitable advertising vectors to get different leads from.

Remember, you don't want to minimize overall cost per lead. You want to maximize overall profits and money in the bank. We'll discuss this more in the later chapter on LTV.

And leadgen can also usually generate more leads than SEO can, which enables more maximum earnings.

So what should your plan be? Ideally sign up for both leadgen and Local SEO together. This will help you get profitable customers now. Then months later you'll get another nice boost in overall profit when the Local SEO kicks into gear. They complement each other well.

You now have a good overview of how Local SEO from a reputable provider can help get you customers down the road and more profitably.

Next, we'll discuss a way to help maximize the number of positive reviews and minimize the number of negative reviews you get.

Exercise:

1. Make sure you read up on Local SEO and traditional SEO, so you have a rough understanding of all the different terms and how it all works.

2. Search out a reputable Local SEO provider in your industry. Find one that provides a realistic timeframe and monthly reports from their tracking methods.

3. Once you're ranked high enough on GMB, invest your surplus earnings into traditional SEO to get your website ranked higher and get more customers that way too.

CHAPTER SEVENTEEN

How To Get A Tidal Wave Of Positive Reviews

"Rob me of my money and you rob me of trash, but rob me of my good name and you make me a poor man indeed."

- Ted Nicholas

Don't you love it when you get a good testimonial?

And don't you hate it when you get a bad review?

Well, in this chapter, we're going to discuss how to maximize the number of positive reviews you get. And help minimize (and defang) the number of negative reviews you get.

In fact, sometimes we can use it to turn an initially bad review into a good review from a now-satisfied customer.

This is what is known as "reputation management."

But first, let's touch on a common subject in advertising: traditional "branding."

What is branding traditionally?

Traditional branding is usually what general advertising agencies try to sell gullible companies that don't know any better. It's focused on making them "appear" more attractive and impressive to potential clients. (Whether they even show this to actual potential clients who have a chance of converting is a whole other topic).

So they charge tens of thousands of dollars to ultimately present the client with a very slick and impressive website (that takes more than 10 seconds to load). They will then dazzle them with very shiny and impressive brochures that are printed on thick card stock. And the grand finale is a giant billboard with the owner looking cool, or something completely irrelevant (it's usually one or the other).

But there's a problem here.

That's not really branding. Not as I want to see it.

And I want to see something that is EFFECTIVE. None of the above is effective at anything other than convincing prospects, that yes, you do run a business.

But is that enough to convince people to buy?

NO! Of course not.

People aren't going to buy from you just because you have a shiny brochure or try to portray yourself as attractive.

In fact, they care less about how you try to present yourself than anything else. They know it's in your best interest to try and portray yourself in the best and most attractive light possible. And this likely includes a hefty amount of exaggeration and deception (and unfortunately sometimes outright lying).

And the other overused "benefit" of that kind of branding is name-recognition. More and more businesses are becoming aware of how little this matters online compared to results. Even back at the height of general advertisers, name-recognition offered little benefits, especially in light of the large costs.

Back when most people used the Yellow Pages to look for businesses to help them, a Bell Atlantic study found 44% were completely uncommitted to any brand. While another 31% had two or more company names in mind, but they were still open-minded. So name-recognition efforts only account for a small minority of potential buyers.

Branding should not be seen as such ineffective methods.

Author Alan Dib has a similar view to mine on branding when he wrote "Branding is something you do after someone has bought from you, rather than something you do to induce them to buy from you."

So I instead want to see branding as what really matters: what others say about you.

Brand is nothing. REPUTATION is everything.

Since what other people say about you is much more believable and trustworthy than anything you could ever say about yourself.

This includes comments and reactions on social media. And of course, it includes the all-mighty customer testimonial.

That's what we are going to try and optimize with reputation management.

Proper reputation-focused branding is great.

And what is that? What is reputation management?

It's a way to help solicit reviews from your customers and then ensure only the best reviews are guided to major review sites.

While any negative reviews are directed to your business, to provide you with the opportunity to reach out and resolve issues any upset customers were having before they have the opportunity to leave a permanent review.

* * *

Fig. 26. You should want to maximize the amount of five-star reviews your business gets.

That's the basic version of reputation management. Let's go deeper.

First, let's look at precisely how reviews affect your business — both for good and ill.

From a study done by Forbes on the effects of positive and negative reviews, we learn several surprising things. Here are the key findings:

- 90% of consumers will read online reviews before visiting a business.

- **74% of consumers say positive reviews help increase their trust in a business.**

- Revenue increases by 5 to 9% for every additional star in a business' rating.

  - Thus, revenue also decreases by 5 to 9% for every single star lost.

- 22% of your customers could be lost if they find a single

negative review on the first page of Google.

- 44% could be lost if they see two negative reviews on the first page of Google.

- 59.2% could be lost if they see three negative reviews on the first page of Google.

- **70% of your customers could be lost if they see four or more negative reviews on the first page of Google.**

- 84% of people trust online reviews as much as a personal recommendation.

I bet some of those stats hit deep.

I was surprised at how impactful reviews were as well. Though when you think about it, it makes sense.

Remember all those infomercials that would run over and over again on TV? Well, the reason they ran over and over again was because they continued to be very profitable over the years. And one of the biggest reasons they were so profitable was that about 70% of the infomercials were dedicated to positive customer testimonials. It reminds me of an online promotion that was about 100 pages long, and over 70 of those pages were dedicated to positive customer testimonials.

Customer reviews have always been powerful sales boosters. That's because they're one of the ultimate forms of proof (and truth) in advertising.

So aside from hope and prayer, how can you help your business generate more positive reviews?

First, you'll want to do an excellent job for your customers. Make them happy and satisfied. That should be priority #1.

Even the best reputation management program can't stop all the negative reviews generated by a bad business. And a bad business isn't likely to get many positive reviews either.

Next, you'll want to sign up for a reputation management service.

Generating reviews is mostly the same across industries. Even industries with restrictions on testimonials are often able to utilize reputation management. Such as the medical industry with HIPAA compliance. Some think it's not possible, but luckily there are ways to make your reputation management HIPAA-compliant. Some services even specialize in it.

I'll explain how reputation management works a little more. It involves setting up a custom page on your website or an external site.

You can direct people to this page with a text or an email, usually sent on the following day. Or you could have your front desk person hand out cards with the page link before they leave.

Or you or anyone at your business, like the front desk person, could schedule a day each week to send out a text or email to all the past customers from that week. You can test each option and figure out which works best for your business type.

When a customer goes to this page, they are asked for a review. Some services use thumbs up or down, while others use a five-star rating system.

I prefer the star ratings as it enables more precise funneling, which I'll explain next.

The customer will choose their rating and then be asked to write about their experience. Then they will submit their review.

Here's where it gets interesting. After they submit their review, there will be different outcomes depending on the rating they gave.

It can be set so if they leave a 4 or 5-star review, they will be thanked and shown additional links. These links will be to major review sites like Google, Facebook, and any industry-specific sites you might use. Most programs will also email them a list of these links too.

This makes it likely they will write a positive review on those sites too.

Are you starting to smile? When I first heard this, I thought it was genius.

But wait, it gets even better!

If they write a 1 to 3-star review, they will first be prompted to write about their grievances and get in contact with you. You are also alerted the second this happens, so you can quickly reach out and make things right. They are still shown the links, since it's against so-called "review gating" compliance rules to hide them. But at least they are much less likely to do anything when you are obviously showing an effort to make things right in their mind.

Don't stop there. Use these 1 to 3-star reviews as opportunities to reach out to try and rectify any issues these customers had with your business.

Now there is a tiny percentage of our population that is horrible and toxic and will get mad about anything. But for the most part, most negative reviews are coming from genuine grievances.

So use each negative review as an opportunity to learn about problems in your business you might have been unaware of. Then fix these problems as soon as possible. This will help prevent future negative reviews. And it will also improve your business to help generate more positive reviews.

Even better, you should reach out to let them know their concerns have been heard. Then lay out the specific changes you'll be making to improve your service for future customers. Thank them for this feedback, and ask what they think would be a fair way to make things right.

This could be anything. Maybe a simple apology. A discount on one of your services. A lesser service for free. And it could go all the way to a full refund.

Bonus: if you can somehow get them back and make them happy (like with a free service offer), then you could potentially turn their initial negative review into a positive review.

In fact, you should be responding to and thanking the positive reviews too. A 2020 study from Brightlocal found 96% of consumers read the responses of businesses to reviews. And 80% of consumers were likely to pick a business that responds to reviews. Even a simple personalized "thank you" is enough. Yet, on average, only 28% of reviews are even responded too.

90% of people are willing to leave reviews, but only 10% of businesses even ask. Let alone use services like reputation management to help maximize their positive reviews.

This ties into SEO as well. The more reviews Google sees you have, the higher they will rank you. And not only for websites on Google, but your Local SEO rank as well.

One other thing it accomplishes is it can often help take the 'fangs' out of any negative reviews that do slip through. We can minimize, but never eliminate all potential negative reviews.

But the ones that slip through will often be less negative than they might have been. That's because they were asked for a review the very next day.

So they weren't allowed to stew about for days or weeks with their grievance until it boiled over and they unleashed their fury on multiple review sites.

Instead, they got it out of their system and moved on with their lives. Hopefully while using your reputation management system, so no one would know it.

You must also consider the fact that online negative reviews might be just the tip of the iceberg of the real amount of bad publicity your business is receiving from angry customers. Except most of it might be happening offline.

Whenever an angry customer has the chance to badmouth your business to someone they know considering your type of services, they won't hesitate to let them know of their poor impression. This can continue to spread over years.

But when you ask for a review immediately, not only do you deflate and minimize the amount of negativity they might spread. You do something much more powerful. You give yourself the opportunity to make things right in the eyes of an upset customer.

So you can do anything from a simple apology for a misunderstanding, to paying what it takes to fix the issue. ie. If you accidentally left an imperceptible amount of dirt on their carpet, you could insist on sending a professional carpet cleaning crew to fix up any areas you might have potentially dirtied. You want to ASTONISH them with your commitment to making things right. And that includes a full refund if that's what it takes.

In fact, all of these options are much less expensive than a single negative reviewer who will continue to badmouth you online and offline for years to come. Just apply the listed statistics above to prove this point.

But it benefits you beyond that. You've not only quashed any perceived slight, but you might have also turned the initial negative review into a positive one. And that again applies offline too. They'll preach the greatness of your business to anyone who'll listen, and people will be impressed at the lengths you'd go to in order to make a customer happy. Even if after reflection it really was just a minor issue.

You might have some existing negative reviews. They might be losing you business right now. If so, then one of the best solutions is to get as many positive reviews as possible. This will help make your most recent reviews look much more attractive.

Prospects will likely have to scroll through many positive reviews before they ever reach a negative review (if they even scroll that far). It will also help bring your average review scores up. Reputation management is especially valuable if you have existing negative reviews.

As an optional service, most providers are also able to reach out to past customers for reviews as well. I'd highly recommend not incentivizing reviews with money or rewards of any sort. This not only goes against the terms of most online platforms, but it's also illegal in many industries.

You're now well aware of how valuable regular positive reviews can be.

Just make sure you use your reputation management service to make these offers. I had a client who insisted on emailing past customers himself. But the problem was he tried emailing them all at once instead of intelligently dripping out the emails at optimal timings, like any reputation management service would automatically do. So the major mail servers suspected that this was spam, and thus the vast majority of the messages didn't get through. So make sure you send these mass requests to past customers through your reputation management service. Usually, they actually send a whole sequence of emails too, usually a few emails over a week or so, to maximize the amount who respond. That is very hard to do and keep track of on your own.

And the bigger problem was we couldn't be sure which ones did get through, so we would have to wait months before a second attempt was possible. Months that could've been made more profitable with more positive reviews.

What else can you do with positive testimonials?

You can post screenshots of them on your social media pages as they come in.

You can even post them on the walls of your business if you operate a physical location where customers walk in. Or even compile a list of them into booklets and leave them in the waiting room. People who leaf through the pages of testimonials might be more willing to follow your advice and even purchase any recommended upsells now that they have seen more of the results of others.

So is there a limit to the effectiveness of positive reviews? There are two factors to this answer.

First, there have been studies showing that even while diminished, there are positive improvements even past 500 reviews for your business.

But the other half of the equation is timing. Searchengineland.com did a study that showed 69% of consumers found reviews irrelevant if they were more than 3 months old. So you'll want both as many positive reviews as possible, along with a regular stream of new reviews.

One of the best reasons to use reputation management is for some people it completely eliminates one of the biggest pain points in running a business. Even more beneficial than the monetary gains is the complete elimination of anxiety and stress some people feel when running a business.

I've talked with business owners aware of the potential damage even a single negative review could cause. And sadly it stressed them out to no end. Even to the point where they tried to hide their business profiles on Google and Facebook so that it would be harder for people to review them, and thus potentially leave a bad review.

Of course, this also made it harder for people to find them period. I hope this chapter is not just a wakeup call for such people, but also a giant relief. You basically just set up this system, and you won't ever have to worry about a single negative review attempt, since you'll have an avalanche of positive reviews to follow and bury it. Of course, that's only if it makes it through before you have a chance to turn it around into a positive experience.

And that's what it's ultimately all about. Improving communication between yourself and your customers to help iterate and improve your business practices to help maximize their happiness.

Reputation management is even more effective when you use the reviews as part of your core marketing strategy to boost the profitability of each marketing service you're using. A 2017 study from Strategic Factory found "the regular use of customer testimonials can help you generate roughly 62% more revenue not only from every customer but from every time they visit your brand."

So this is why it's effective to harness reviews generated from reputation management. They can increase the profitability of indirect marketing services like Social Media Management, as well as more direct marketing services like Lead Generation and Local SEO. And it works the other way too. Those services help improve your reputation management performance by providing you with a bigger stream of customers to generate reviews from.

You now have a good understanding of what branding is and what branding isn't. You've learned the statistics showing how valuable having regular positive reviews is, and how detrimental to your business negative reviews can be. You see how reputation management can help you maximize the number of positive reviews you get. And you'll take action by doing everything you can to make your customers happy in the first place.

Next, we'll discuss a way to make social media profitable instead of a time sink.

Exercise:

1. Make sure your customers are happy and satisfied. This is priority #1. Make any changes to ensure this is the case going forward.

2. Sign up for reputation management.

3. Ensure each customer is given the link to your review page. Either from a text or email sent the following day, or by your front desk giving them a card with the link. Or you could upload a list of your customers from that week on a weekly basis.

4. Immediately follow up with negative reviews to help make things right in their minds. Also reply to positive reviews expressing thanks.

5. Use the feedback from negative (and positive) reviews to help make valuable improvements in your business.

CHAPTER EIGHTEEN

Social Media: Time Sink Or Opportunity?

Social Media.

Is it the ultimate time sink or the greatest marketing opportunity?

Honestly, it's a lot more of the former. At least for most businesses.

Remember the circle exercise I had you do, where you circled the business tasks only you could do? After talking with your new TOP5 contacts, I'm sure you also realized these were also probably the most profitable activities you could do.

Your most profitable tasks are likely performing the most vital services of your business, and actually closing prospects too. So your job should be to max out your time spent doing those things.

Once you're successful enough, you could delegate these tasks too. Like when a dentist hires other dentists to work at their clinic. Going further, you could make your business turn-key then franchise it. You could do the same thing over multiple locations.

But sadly most business owners don't have this grand vision (or any vision at all). They think they are making progress by diddling around on Twitter all day making posts and getting into fights.

Then you look at their schedule and see it's pretty barren. They have few to no appointments.

Their problem is focus. A problem you now are eliminating thanks to the circle exercise.

* * *

Fig. 27. Various Social Media platforms. Image Credit: Wikimedia Commons by   Ibrahim.ID CC-BY-SA 4.0

That's not to say social media is entirely useless, far from it.

When you spend a small fraction of your income on hiring experienced professionals to manage it, you can get a positive return on your income.

They can set up and manage your profiles. Create valuable posts and tweets. Some can even write articles and other valuable content related to your business.

The big value of this is it helps prospects who are taking a look at your business online see you're active on social media. And thus you look like an active legitimate business. Unlike your competitors who last posted weeks, months, or even YEARS ago. And whose pages look dead and barren.

One reason to keep an occasional eye on social media is to read the modern equivalent of your "white mail." In the past, white mail meant the letters you were sent by customers and prospects, giving you feedback. While you might still get them even now, the modern variation might be tweets or Facebook comments.

They can be useful food for thought. You don't have to act on every piece of feedback, but you'll get a better feel of where your business is.

They help you feel the 'pulse' of your business.

Exposing areas that could use improvement. And so on.

Let's start by looking at the Facebook social media platform.

Most businesses would benefit from at least having an active business fan page on Facebook. That's even if you don't get most of your customers from Facebook directly. Remember that statistic from the reputation management chapter: "90% of consumers will read online reviews before visiting a business." And those consumers will check out your reviews and profile on Facebook as part of their investigation.

If they see few reviews and no recent posts, (or worse, no Facebook business page at all), then they will find your business less credible than it could otherwise be. And your competition is probably not leaving that kind of money on the table.

You should be aiming to make at least one post a day on Facebook. One post a week is basically the bare minimum to not appear like a potentially dead and abandoned business. These posts could be video testimonials. Pictures of before and afters, or other completed projects. Maybe snapshots of written testimonials from other websites. And even just interesting and entertaining content related to your industry.

You should follow up with comments and messages as soon as you're able. This turbo-drives both the natural engagement, such as likes, shares, comments, and views. But it also gives a you a further boost to your post's exposure from that platform's algorithm. This is because it rightly thinks your post is valuable and should be shown to more people.

It's especially important to reply to comments and messages when you're doing a Facebook leadgen program. That's because the people you're paying to show ads to will be more likely to click if they see you actively engaging with comments of others. On the other hand, if they see 5 other commenters asking the same question with no reply from the business, then they'll think that business doesn't care about them. So they'll be less likely to convert.

And this all creates a sort of multiplier effect since the main benefit of engagement is every single friend and follower of each engager can see it when they like, share, or comment on a post. With enough engagement, this can multiply the organic reach of your social media posts and ads.

It's helpful if you install the "Facebook Pages Manager" app on your phone (or ideally the phone of whomever handles communications at your business). This will let you be notified the second a prospect comments on your post or messages you. Then you can make them happy with a quick response (outside of your Do Not Disturb hours).

And of course, hide & ban & delete any negative comments.

I recommend all my clients do this. Again, you can also have an employee with Facebook Page access do it on their phone.

* * *

.ull 🤍　　　　　　2:04 PM　　　　　　▬

☰　　　　Messages ▾　　　💬✓　　Q

　　(●)　　　　(f)　　　　(◆)　　　　(◎)

Nicolas Vilabos
You: Hi Nicolas, it's been a ... · Tue　　⭐

Natalie Page
Awesome, thanks!　· Tue
● VIP

Marco Muji
Yes! It comes with a cotton... · Tue
● New Customer

Emily Gregson
You: Take a look and let ...· Mon

Sarah Pei
You: Sorry they're a limit...· Mon　　⭐

Amy Barber
You: Thank you! · Sun
● VIP

Lila Dudley
You: Thank you! · Sun

Bruno Frisk
What's your address · Sun

🗒　　📈　　🗄　　🔔　　🗓　　💼

Fig. 28. Example screenshot of Facebook Pages Manager app. Image Credit: Facebook Inc.

Here's a quick tip on how to block any scammers or negative people from commenting on your Facebook ads and posts. Go into your business Facebook Page settings and click the word "Edit." It's beside the section titled something similar to "Page Moderation." It will show something like "Posts containing these words will be blocked."

You can use this to help block the tiny percentage of spammers and negative losers from making negative comments on your Facebook ads and posts. While they are rare, these comments can still hurt your conversion rate. It hides comments containing any of the blacklisted words you specify. Then only their friends will be allowed to see the comments, and no one else.

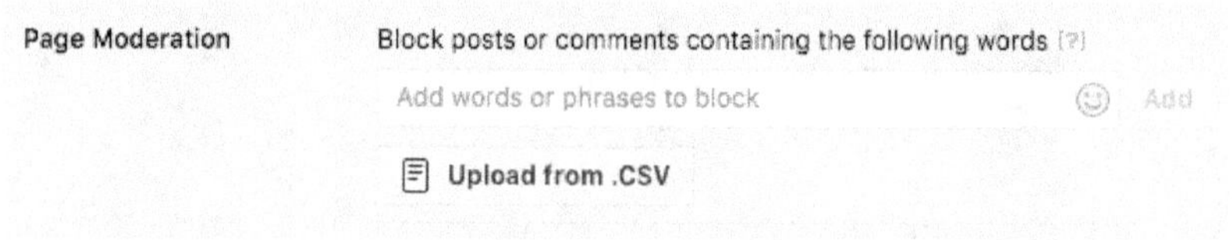

Page Moderation   Block posts or comments containing the following words [?]

Add words or phrases to block   ☺   Add

🖹 Upload from .CSV

Fig. 29. Facebook Page Moderation blacklist. Found under your page settings.

Blacklist words like:
- Ebay
- Amazon
- www
- http
- https
- ://
- Sucks
- Aliexpress

- Expensive
- High
- Price
- Thieves
- Scam
- Scammers
- China
- No way
- Ripoff
- Rippoff
- Beware
- Make these
- Make this
- How long
- Charge
- Legit
- Paypal
- Sketchy
- Hidden
- Leery
- Leary
- Scared
- Don't trust
- Dont trust
- BS
- Low life
- Creep

I'm sure there are other negative words more commonly used in your industry. Include those too.

For all other negative or spammy comments that get through, you should tap the three dots next to their comment. Then tap "Hide comment." Then tap "Ban [user]." Then tap "Delete comment."

There, that's it.

Now you can move on and keep your focus on the positive prospects and customers you have, without any worry or bad vibes from the losers out there.

To clarify, this only applies to obviously negative comments. If someone has a genuine question like "how much does this cost?" or "what is your availability like?" I'd recommend answering these questions to provide value to future prospects who view these exchanges.

While it's a grey area, I'd still consider questions like "Do I really have to submit my email? I don't like sharing my email" to be negative.

Now if possible, I'd be vague with questions regarding cost, and tell them you'd have to find out more about their situation and needs. Tell them they should submit their info to give you a better idea of how you can help. You don't want to spoil every detail upfront before they even see your full offer. Tell them to click the link and submit their information to find out.

You can also set your "Profanity Filter" in your Facebook Page Settings to Strong (or medium if you are in a generally profane niche). This can help filter out any more negative comments your blacklist might miss.

If you find your posts or ads aren't getting many comments or engagement, I'd recommend commenting yourself. Post a comment like "Please share if you know anyone interested in this." That should help grease the wheels for future comments.

These are the important points to keep in mind for Facebook. Again, Facebook is valuable for any business type as a way for the 90% of prospects who check you out to confirm you're an active business with good reviews.

Where the benefits of social media gets murky is when it comes to the other social media platforms.

My general safe recommendation is to at the very least sign up on every single major social media platform (which I'll cover below). Another advantage of signing up everywhere is it makes it harder for someone to sign up on there pretending to be you.

And then have your Social Media Management provider push copies of your posts to those platforms. And this should include any required tweaks to optimize each post for each platform. ie. Some platforms have character limits, other platforms are optimized for video, etc.

The advantage of this strategy is over time you'll get a general impression of how well the audiences of each platform respond and engage with your business type and post content. You'll see some platforms just don't seem to care at all.

While other platforms might have people happily engaging with and subscribing to your content. This is great. Then you'll know to invest more time and social media energy on those platforms. You should also at least download the corresponding apps too, so you'll be able to more quickly respond to comments and messages.

And when you're doing especially well on a platform, it's definitely worth at least testing some advertising on there. That's because it will likely be more profitable than on platforms that aren't producing organic engagements.

Entire series of books could be written on all the ins and outs of each social media platform, but I'm going to go through each in a rapid-fire style. And only touch on the most important suggestions. These are all the platforms you should be signed up on:

Facebook: get a professional headshot for your profile photo, and pay a professional graphic designer for a custom cover image with your logo.

GMB: while technically not true social media, it's just as important as Facebook to have a verified profile on. Make sure you or your manager is making regular posts as posts disappear after a week.

LinkedIn: fill out all areas of your profile, and try to inject your USP into both your main description and the brief description below your name. Also hire a professional graphic designer to make you a cover image.

Instagram: look up the $1.80 Instagram strategy and thank me later.

Twitter: hire a professional graphic designer to make you a cover image. You'll likely have to tweak your post content to fit within the character limit.

Snapchat: focus on showing the more human side of your business. It's all about "KLT" on this platform. That is, using it to help people Know, Like, and Trust you more.

Pinterest: essential if your primary market is made up of women. As of 2021, 60% of the platform's users were women. Though the male/female gap is gradually shrinking over time.

TikTok: some businesses can benefit from TikTok. Just be sure to post daily and keep your videos around 15 seconds.

Reddit (and industry forums): be careful. Most people from Reddit and industry forums abhor all types of advertising. But you can still take advantage of it by trying to be helpful in the right subreddits and forum sections. Ideally with stories related to how you solved a relevant problem for someone... maybe only mentioning your business if someone asks.

* * *

Those are the major platforms to sign up on.

Again, to make this all easier, you'll want to take advantage of Social Media Management (SMM). It helps get more people engaged with your content. Those engaged people can be more easily targeted to show your future offers. They're showing you they are hotter prospects.

SMM also encourages engagement on these platforms. And when someone engages with your content, these platforms are more likely to show your ads to them, which makes your ads more profitable.

Some platforms, like GMB, even have their posts expire after a week. So SMM is another easy guaranteed way to secure more Google real estate for your own business.

When you look at all the data and recommendations from social media gurus, the number one most important recommendation to maximize your success on any social media platform is to post consistently. That's it. And SMM puts this all-important task on autopilot for you.

You'll find SMM to be another way to create value for your business. And more importantly, it will let you buy more time to do your most profitable tasks, like directly closing people.

Another advantage of SMM is when it comes to generating additional "touches" from your business. If you can recall back to the chapter with the HBR study, it found the more 'touches' you make with each lead, the more likely they are to convert. Touches can be call attempts, emails, text messages, and voicemails. But they can also include likes, shares, comments, and other forms of engagement with your social media. And the touches are especially valuable when you directly touch them back by replying to their messages, and replying or engaging with their comments.

These touches all help prime prospects to be more likely and easier to convert when they encounter your other marketing efforts. This could be when viewing your lead generation offer, or when they find your SEO-boosted business at the top of a Google search.

And here's one last way you can make social media run 100% on autopilot, so you can spend your time doing things only you can do and which bring in the most profit. You might already have someone managing some of your communications like making and taking calls, texts, and emails for your business. Maybe it is your front desk person at a physical location, or even a virtual assistant that specializes in communications and conversions.

Well, in addition to using SMM for content marketing to generate engagement, you can also assign your communications person to respond to comments and messaging on these platforms. This is often more effective than doing it yourself, since you might be busy closing a client or doing a project. And thus they'd be more likely to respond more quickly. And from what we learned from the HBR chapter, the more quickly you can respond, the more you wow and astonish your prospects, and thus the higher your conversion rate will be.

You now have an idea of how to make your social media more profitable with SMM. Next, we'll discuss your "LTV" and how knowing it can help you maximize the number of customers you can afford.

Exercise:

1.   If you're generating leads on Facebook, download the "Facebook Pages Manager" app to your phone.

2.   Promptly reply to any comments or messages to your Facebook posts and ads. The more helpful your responses are, the more eager prospects who see these exchanges will be to work with you.

3.   Hide & Ban & Delete any negative or spammy comments. Get them out of your life.

4.   Setup your Page Moderation blacklist on your Facebook Page settings to further reduce spammy and negative comments.

5.   Set your Profanity Filter on your Facebook Page settings to

medium to further reduce spammy and negative comments.

6. Sign up on every major social media platform mentioned in this chapter. At the very least, it will help prevent people from pretending to be your business.

7. Use the tips for each platform to help you maximize your results on each, and over time figure out which platforms give you the most positive engagement and future customers. Then focus your social media time and energy on those platforms.

8. Hire a Social Media Management service to manage your social media for you. This will help provide valuable content to your prospects and show you're an active business.

9. If and when you have hired someone else at your business to be in charge of communications, like a front desk person, put them in charge of also responding to comments and messages on social media. Then you won't risk wasting a single second on being sucked into social media, and you can invest your time into activities that help realize your vision as soon as possible.

CHAPTER NINETEEN

How To Get Every Possible Customer & Dollar (And Referral)

What is LTV?

And how can LTV help you figure out how to get maximum customers, so you can leapfrog your competition?

This important concept is rarely talked about in business. Yet it's essential for helping you figure out how to maximize the number of customers you can get.

LTV generally stands for "Average Lifetime Customer Value."

It refers to what an average customer of yours is worth to you over their lifetime after subtracting business expenses.

If they all pay you one time and then never see you again, then your LTV will be that single payment.

However, if they continue to buy from you again and again, then your LTV will increase.

The more frequently they buy from you, the higher your LTV.

The more they pay for your different products and services, the higher your LTV.

And the longer they continue to buy from you over future months or years, the higher your LTV.

Some customers will only buy from you once, while others will buy from you many times and over the years. You only care about the average, which is what LTV calculates.

If you have a referral program, then you can include the value of the average number of generated referrals per customer in your LTV too.

I've listed the steps to get a rough calculation of your LTV. They're in the exercise at the end of this chapter.

This is another reason why you should be using a CRM system. It will allow you to keep track of every customer and their individual payments over the years. This would help you calculate your precise LTV for this moment in time.

For now, what's important is figuring out how to increase it — and figuring out how to use it to get maximum incoming customers.

To increase it, I'd recommend talking with your new TOP5 friends to help brainstorm ideas. I'm sure they can help you find ways to get your current customers paying more and coming back more. There are different strategies for each industry, so your TOP5 friends will have a good idea of what you can do.

Next, figure out how much on average it costs you to get a customer. Get a very rough estimate by dividing the number of new customers you got last year from your advertising budget. (If you have a referral program, then add its budget to your ad budget when dividing).

Hopefully, the average cost to get a new customer is lower than your LTV.

If it isn't, then you need to quickly find out from your TOP5 contacts how to increase your LTV. Also, drop any advertising sources that aren't getting you any customers. If particular advertising sources you're using aren't using website link-tracking. And if they aren't using a call-tracking number or coupon code, or etc to track and measure their results, then they likely aren't getting you any.

The secret genius idea in this chapter is the fact you can spend up to your LTV to get a new customer, and still make a profit.

And if you increase your LTV, you are then able to spend even more to acquire a new customer.

Am I saying you should break even with all your advertising? Not at all.

What I'm saying is you likely have a list of advertising 'vectors' you could potentially pay to get new customers from.

These advertising vectors might consist of:

- Facebook advertising
- Google advertising
- Local SEO
- Website SEO
- Dream 100
- Social Media Management
- Reputation management
- Email advertising
- LinkedIn advertising
- Internet-wide retargeting
- Local Newspaper advertising
- Local TV advertising
- Local Magazine advertising
- Industry-specific Magazine advertising
- Local influencer endorsements on social media
- Your Referral program
- Etc.

It costs different amounts to generate customers from each of these vectors.

And what your mission should be is to:

1. Figure out which vectors cost less to get a customer than your current LTV.

2. Rank them from the most profitable vector to the least

profitable (yet still profitable) vector.

3.   One by one, max out your investment in each vector, starting with the most profitable ones.

Taking these steps will get you maximum profit from the most profitable vectors to the least profitable.

And this of course includes free options that are especially important when you're just starting out. Options like calling, emailing, or messaging your friends and family on social media to see if they know people you could help. This doesn't cost a dime.

When it came to my own business, I was surprised by the results.

Of all the ad testing, I expected the best performing to be LinkedIn ads. That's because I work in the B2B arena by helping businesses get more customers. Though it turned out after actually testing each vector, that I got the highest ROI from Facebook ads.

For some business types, it cost me less than $3 per sales call. While on other advertising platforms, it might cost me dozens or even hundreds of dollars per call.

Of course, even some of those higher cost-per-call vectors were still profitable. That's because I calculated my LTV before I started testing and tracking the different advertising vectors. And found even some of the high cost per call vectors were still profitable across an average customer's lifetime.

Some businesses make the mistake of not investing in the less profitable vectors to minimize advertising. Or worse they invest only in the highest-ROI vector, yet still try to minimize their investment in it. Your goal shouldn't be to minimize advertising. It should be to MAXIMIZE MONEY IN THE BANK. Maximize profits. Period.

When you boil it down, the real problem might be some people just AREN'T GREEDY ENOUGH. Not when they prioritize "FREE" options or paying as little as possible even when it's counter-productive. And penny-pinching in other ways both in their business and in life itself.

I've already given plenty of examples in the time management chapter, such as those who operate on themselves with a dental kit for dogs. You don't see Warren Buffet or Elon Musk doing that. But I'm going to emphasize the most important and undeniable lesson here:

There's only so much money you can save, while there's an UNLIMITED amount of money you can make.

So prioritize using your time and investments to MAKE as much money as possible. Stop trying to save a few trees when you can focus on growing an additional forest.

After maxing out your investment in the most profitable ad vectors, invest in the remaining vectors that are still profitable. Go out there and take those profits. This will also take them away from your competition too.

Many businesses, even major ones who are (or were) on the Fortune-500 list, restrict themselves by using an arbitrary advertising budget. ie. Only 20% of their budget will go into advertising.

This doesn't make any sense.

If you could buy $5 bills for only $2, would you limit the number of bills you could buy to only 20% of your budget? NO WAY! You'd want to MAX OUT the number of bills you could buy until it ceased to be profitable. That's what effective advertising really is: buying dollars at a discount.

If your advertising dollars are generating a positive ROI, then you should MAX IT OUT. Starting by maxing out the most profitable vectors.

ie. Max out buying the $5 bills from the $2 source, then from the $3 source, then from the $4 source, and so on. It certainly beats the return from investing in the stock market.

Then max out less and less profitable vectors until you can't make any more profit without increasing your LTV further.

ie. Once you've bought from every source more profitable, then you should still buy the $5 bills from the $4.99 source.

In this example, doubling your LTV would be the same thing as turning the $5 bills into $10 bills. Then you could buy them from every source costing less than $9.99 per bill and still make additional profit.

And so on.

This leads us into the most striking benefits of LTV.

By increasing your LTV, you can multiply the total NUMBER of profitable customers available to you.

It's not only about increasing profitability per customer. And it's also not only about making previously unprofitable vectors now profitable.

But it's also about increasing the TOTAL audience of people on the planet you can profitably reach and market to. Since not everyone is available on every marketing vector or platform. So as you make more and more vectors profitable, you are able to expose yourself to more and more of the people who would buy from you.

And some people just don't seem to convert on specific platforms for whatever reason. But when they see you somewhere else, maybe somewhere where your niche doesn't traditionally advertise because their lower LTV didn't make it profitable, then such prospects might be more open to converting.

In addition to generating every cent possible there's another advantage to spending up to your LTV to get another customer. It's based on the fact that usually your LTV is increasing. As you add more services and reasons for people to come back more and more over time, and gradually increase your perceived value, your LTV will naturally increase.

So the customers you bought at break-even prices will gradually become more and more profitable.

There are other ways to further improve your arithmetic with these advertising vectors. For example, by implementing a reputation management program to generate more positive reviews along with an SMM program to show you're an active business that cares by providing valuable content and engagement, you'll convert a higher percentage of people who'll check you out from the various vectors.

As you get more and more positive reviews, not only will these vectors be more and more profitable, but you'll be able to retest other vectors that previously weren't profitable and see if your cost per conversion has gone down enough so that it's now profitable to advertise through.

One way to add more profitable products and services is to think of your business as a "Value Ladder." Not every customer is the same. 20% of your customers might be willing to pay for a service that costs 5X as much. And 5% of your customers might be willing to pay for a service that costs 20X as much. 20% of 5 is 1, and 5% of 20 is 1.

So by adding these additional services to your existing service (1), you could basically triple your LTV (1 + 20% of 5 + 5% of 20 = 3).

Now, these are just rough guidelines. It doesn't have to be exactly 5X more or 20X more, or expect exactly 20% and so on. But they are within the ballpark of the results many businesses see when they have an increasing ladder of additional services this way.

How do you brainstorm and find these additional higher-priced products and services? Just ask your TOP5 friends. Also, see what the most profitable businesses in your industry are doing. You'll likely come away with many ideas.

And you don't have to limit yourself to 5X or 20X. You could do 0.5X, 1.3X, 2X, 13X, 100X, etc. Model the high prices your TOP5 friends and the most profitable businesses are using.

Don't think, "no one will ever pay that much for this service." If the most profitable businesses have something priced that way, then you can be sure at least SOMEONE finds it valuable enough to pay for.

* * *

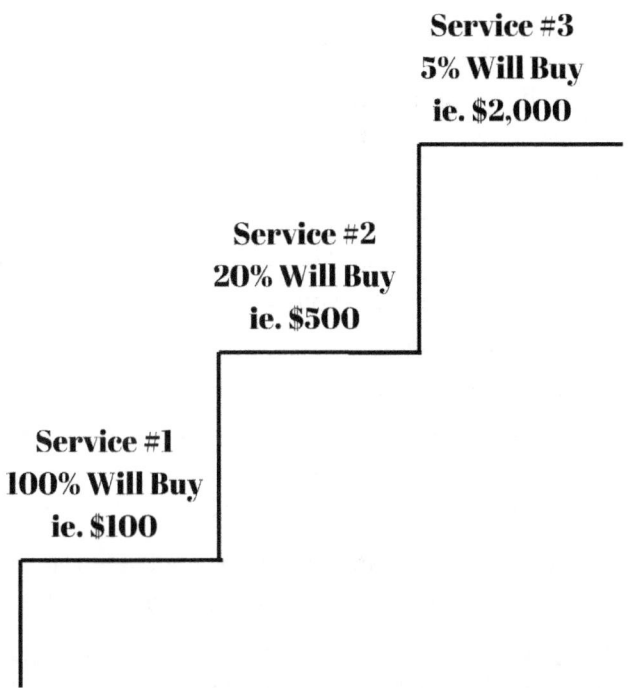

Fig. 30. Example Value Ladder.

Next, let's quickly touch on having a dedicated referral program. Now what is that and how can it help you increase your LTV?

Let's look at the system most people use to generate referrals: hope.

Maybe with a bit of prayer.

Some might even try to do a 'good job.'

And other brave souls might go even further and actually ask for referrals.

Most people like to think of referrals as bonus free money.

But after reading enough of this book, I bet you can feel there's a better way. And there is.

Your goal should not be to merely get bonus money out of people referred to your business. You should instead try to MAXIMIZE the amount of money you can get by generating referrals.

First of all, if you're not already doing this, you should let every new customer know you get a lot of your business from referrals. And tell them you'd be happy if they would send more people your way.

Next, you should figure out how much you'll now be paying on average to get a customer from your various tested vectors.

The secret is then to allow yourself to spend up to that amount to get a new referred customer.

Say it costs $200 on average to generate a new customer from advertising. Then you should be willing to pay up to $200 to generate each new customer from referrals.

This will help you max out the number of referrals you could possibly get, and thus maximize your profit from referrals.

One way you can start spending money today is by sending your current customers gifts. Here's an example of this from the real estate industry:

The real estate guru Brian Buffini recommends realtors do monthly 'pop-by's with a small gift to the homes of past customers. This involved presenting them with a thoughtful gift like dog-biscuits from a dog bakery for customers with dogs, Peeps marshmallows around Easter, ketchup/mustard/relish pack during BBQ season, an environmentally-friendly shopping bag, etc. And each gift was paired with a tailored call-to-action asking for more referrals.

A great example of the success of this is one of his students did 150 pop-bys a month and consistently generated eight new referrals a month. And remember these were referrals that might spend hundreds of thousands or even millions on a home.

Though doing pop-bys is usually best for niches with few, yet very profitable customers, like realtors. For non-realtors who deal with many times more new customers every month, you'd probably be better off sticking with mailed gifts or gifts given at your place of business.

Beyond surprise gifts, you could spend your referral budget on:

- Monthly contests with prizes awarded to those who referred the most customers.

- Gift cards sent to every customer who generated a new referral.

- Welcome packages to every new customer.

- A monthly newsletter.

- Events.

- Etc.

A quick guideline is to ask yourself what are the best gifts and rewards your competitors are sending their customers. Then aim to at least beat those gifts.

Depending on your industry and the legalities involved, and the companies and policies involved, you could even reward people directly with cash or gift cards for each successful referral. But again, first make sure it's legal for you to do this and doesn't go against company policy of either your company or the company your referring person works at.

I love sending out direct cash and gift card rewards whenever possible to generate referrals for my own marketing company. That's because it's one of the best ways to help motivate continued future referrals.

There's another secret reason you should be willing to pay up to the average cost to get a customer in order to generate a referral. That's because referrals are generally WORTH MORE than customers you get from non-referral sources. This is since referrals generally buy more from you, are less price-sensitive, and also do business with you longer.

And on that note, the money you invest with present customers to generate referrals from also usually has a positive impact on their retention rate. So they'll tend to do business with you longer, and thus their LTV will increase.

You sort of get a 2-for-1 deal for both retention and referrals with an optimized dedicated referral program.

Now, can you see how profitable knowing and increasing your LTV can be?

By maxing out your LTV and then maxing out all the customers you get from advertising and your referral program, you will easily leapfrog all your local competition and beyond.

You might be wondering, once you've maxed out your business with new customers, where can you go from there?

Hire more staff to take on more new customers.

Make your business as turn-key as possible.

Hire a general manager to take over from you.

Franchise your business all over the country and beyond. Do it by using the profitable systems and strategies you've learned from this book. Your competition likely isn't capitalizing on many of these ideas at all. The book "The E-Myth" talks further about this franchising strategy.

After all, successful marketer Ted Nicholas recommends the day you should start planning on selling your business is the day you start your business. Remember for each dollar you add to your yearly income, you will be adding a multiple of that to the present value of your business.

So let's say you invest in every LTV vector that's profitable. Not only will you suck up every customer and dollar of income possible now, but you'll also get multiples of that additional yearly income when you want to sell your business. If this concept seems too amazing to believe, then just talk to any one of your TOP5 friends that've sold a business before. They'll leave you with a big smile.

And of course these are all ideas on the business end of things. You can apply the same sort of ideas to your personal investments with the money you've earned from maxing out your business earnings. Maybe stocks, bonds, real estate, property management, crypto, etc. Hire and ask a financial manager first before making any such investments.

You now know how to find, increase, and use your LTV to maximize the number of customers you can afford. And you will also use the same ideas to maximize the amount of referrals you'll generate.

Next, we'll look at a way to identify and convert a list of your best potential customers.

Exercise:

1. Calculate your LTV.

    -   A rough way to calculate it is to find the amount of profit you made over the last year (not including advertising), then divide that by the number of unique paying customers you saw over the previous year (if you can't, then guess).

    -   This is your base 1-year average customer value.

    -   Then figure out the percentage of customers who use your services over 2-years. Increase your LTV by this percentage.

    -   Then figure out the percentage of customers who use your services over 3-years. Increase your LTV by this percentage.

    -   And continue to do this until you run out of years.

    -   You should now have a rough idea of your LTV.

    -   Ideally, you will be tracking all individual customers and their payments using your CRM over the years to get a precise number for where your LTV is this very month (since it's usually increasing over time).

2. Talk with your new TOP5 friends to brainstorm ways to increase your LTV. Find ways to charge more (perhaps with additional services), make people return more frequently, and make them remain a customer for a longer period of time.

3. Know you can spend up to your LTV to get a new customer, and still make a profit.

4. Use this to maximize the number of customers you can get, vacuuming out your region, and starving your competition. Start with the most profitable vectors (found from testing), and work your way down.

5. Create a dedicated referral program and apply these same ideas to maximize the amount of referrals you generate.

CHAPTER TWENTY

The Secret To Winning Your Dream Customers

We've been discussing ways to bring in lots of customers so far. But what if instead you'd like to focus on fewer customers?

Why would you ever consider that?

Maybe you're in an industry with a small yet lucrative set of potential customers. ie. If you have a service that specifically helps Fortune 500 CEOs, then by definition you technically only have a market of 500 people. But on the other hand, each one of these customers might be good for deals of hundreds of thousands or even millions in yearly revenue.

Or more likely, you're a common business type that can serve a wide range of people. Perhaps you'd like to laser focus on a tiny yet lucrative part of your market.

An example might be an electrical contractor. On the residential side of things, they might have many nearby homes they could help with construction, repairs, or lighting upgrades. But maybe they'd prefer to focus on getting the fewer yet more lucrative commercial opportunities. Perhaps doing major lighting and wiring projects for local commercial businesses.

But the problem is there are much fewer commercial opportunities than residential. And maybe only a small subset of those commercial companies are ones you know you could help.

In either type of scenario, what could you do to get these small groups of prospects to become some of your most lucrative customers?

The answer lies in the concept of the Dream 100.

I learned the earliest published variant of it might have been a part of the early Ford Motor Company encouraging its sales force to identify and concentrate on a list of most-likely buyers of Ford vehicles.

This idea likely spread out and has become practiced in a variety of industries since. Though it didn't become fully fleshed out and publicized until the famous advertiser, David Ogilvy, finally wrote about it.

His idea was to write down a list of the hundred businesses he'd most like to have as clients for his advertising business, Ogilvy & Mather. He called this list his 'Dream 100.'

He'd then put in some effort every day into regularly soliciting business from among these companies. Not contacting every company on every day, but spreading it out over every week or so.

From letters to phone calls, and with help from his office, he made every attempt to provide value to various representatives of these companies. This was in order to build relationships and get closer and closer with setting up meetings with decision-makers that might be willing to give him a chance.

And he claimed it worked so well, that he considered this Dream 100 strategy one of the best ways to generate business.

So how does it all work?

There are six key steps in applying your own Dream 100 strategy:

1. Choose your Dream 100 customers.
2. Choose the lumpy segues you mail them.
3. Create your prospecting letters (yes, letters, NOT email).
4. Create your calendar.
5. Make follow-up calls based on the calendar.

6.   Set up a meeting to pitch each prospect.

Let's go through each one by one.

First, you make your list of Dream 100 customers. This might be a small subsection of your market that is especially lucrative. A good example might be local companies that employ a lot of people. You'll want your list to be made of prospects that are a combination of lucrative, yet easy enough and fun.

You will regularly reach out to each list prospect with the ultimate goal of getting in front of them and pitching your unique offer for them. Sometimes it's hard to figure out who the best person to contact is, especially at larger companies. So some of this reaching out will involve figuring out who the real decision-makers are. The ones who are able to hire and pay you. So focus on getting a meeting with them.

You'll then brainstorm unique offers you can try to present them with, ideally in combination with the USP you figured out in the USP chapter. If you can't brainstorm anything, then at the very least your USP and standard services are what you should try to present.

An example of a unique offer might be a local chiropractor trying to solicit corporate clients by offering a free seminar (at least free the first time) on optimal posture and reducing carpal tunnel syndrome in the workplace. Plus as many free adjustments afterward as time allows. And of course offering maybe one free future adjustment for each employee, or some sort of irresistible offer to get them to come in.

And of course they'd want to make the offer as valuable as possible, so they could be invited back over and over again.

But again, it doesn't have to be fancy. It could be your normal pitch to every client, but hopefully now incorporating your USP. The difference is you'd now be in front of your most ideal prospect, instead of just an average one.

Then you will want to try to contact them usually via a combination of letter mail and follow-up calls. Now you might be thinking: "Why put in time to write letter mail when everyone uses email these days? Also who even reads letter mail these days anyway?"

The answer is few people send or receive letter mail, which is what makes it so impactful. Tons of people receive tons of email too, and the vast majority of it ends up in the spam folder or deleted. So if you want to be noticed and have your correspondence actually read, then at least use letter mail.

Sometimes letter mail isn't even enough. In the earlier example of trying to contact Fortune 500 CEOs, you won't have any hope of getting anything that isn't Fed-Ex'd to them read. In fact, at that level you might even consider more impactful ideas. Ideas like having your message delivered in a gold-plated briefcase handcuffed to a Brinks Security courier.

Now that would be excessive for most industries. But if you're pitching something that could be responsible for hundreds of thousands or even millions of additional yearly revenue, you can start really calculating what you can afford to invest at that level of prospecting.

But again, for most people, a letter is enough. Though there is a secret way we can make that more impactful: relevant gifts you can segue.

These don't have to be expensive gifts, just RELEVANT. By that I mean you can make an excuse to segue the gift from your letter to your offer.

For the chiropractor example, this might be an aspirin tablet to segue into you helping reduce employee pain from carpal tunnel syndrome and non-optimal posture.

For the electrical contractor, this might be an LED bulb segueing into helping modernize their lighting and wiring to save costs.

For a financial planner, this might be some foreign currency that has suffered from hyperinflation due to poor financial planning.

And so on.

And as I was hinting at earlier, the best advantage of this is it usually helps make your letter mail look and feel more lumpy. Some in the marketing industry refer to this as "lumpy mail." And they refer to the segue items as "grabbers" (as in attention-grabbers).

This makes your letter much more likely to be both noticed and opened, so that they can find out what's inside.

You should be sending these letters with different grabbers every 2 to 4 weeks to each prospect on your Dream 100 list, followed by a follow-up call. Now, you don't have to include a grabber in every letter. For example, you could send a copy of your monthly newsletter in another. But including grabbers is the only way to almost guarantee they'll be read.

Try to write a list of some creative segues for your industry. Then you can test them over the months you test mailing them out.

You should try to keep this all organized with some sort of calendar to track who should be sent letters and follow-up calls on each date. You might even be able to do this with your CRM using a special segmentation.

On each follow-up call, your goal is always to inch your way closer to getting in contact with the real decision-maker. Then once in contact, schedule a meeting to pitch your offer.

As mentioned in the sales chapter, you could incorporate your daily Dream 100 calls in the morning. You can make them right after your calls to any leads that came in after hours. (Again, BEFORE any email). That way you'll do them consistently and they'll actually get done.

This could take months of Dream 100 prospecting to get a meeting with each prospect, or sometimes a couple of weeks. You can certainly help speed up the process by utilizing services such as reputation management and SMM.

Since, like 90% of other prospects, your Dream 100 list members WILL check you out. And they're much more likely to be open to and prioritize hearing your pitch if they see lots of happy recent reviews with proven results, along with an active social media with people happily engaging with your company and content.

But with either timeframe, your goal is to stick it out for the long haul. That's because even a year's worth of correspondence with a company adds up to just 26 phone calls and 26 letters if you're doing it every other week. And again, this is to solicit some of your most lucrative and ideal clients.

Then once you get in front of them, just pitch your offer while emphasizing your USP. You won't convert everyone, but you'll be very happy with your overall results.

And one of the best parts of getting these higher-end "dream" clients is you can then apply your referral program to them. Then they'll be more likely to refer similar high-end clients.

Going back to our original example, wanna know one of the best ways to get in contact with a Fortune 500 CEO? It's simple, just get a referral from another Fortune 500 CEO.

No Brinks courier nor handcuffed golden briefcase necessary.

I will say you can incorporate both email and social media outreach into this process, but only as additional vectors after the mandatory letters and calls. Most people are naturally lazy and inclined to try and just put the entire list on a monthly email sequence and call it a day. That doesn't have nearly the same level of impact nor effectiveness. Especially not with your highest-valued prospects.

I hope you've appreciated my attempts to force you to see the impact and value of lumpy mail and calls.

It might not be obvious at first, but this could apply to almost any business.

Let's use a hard example of a guy with a food truck business downtown. His product, and only product, is $1 grilled-cheese-and-butter sandwiches. (This is actually based on the idea of Daniel Danger who dreamed of selling $1 grilled-cheese sandwiches, which inspired real food trucks with this model).

Let's make it extra-challenging and pretend they're not even using social media or any of the other strategies mentioned in this book.

* * *

Fig. 31. The $1 Grilled Cheese food truck example. Image credit: Brett Sayles

So how is he supposed to apply Dream 100 when he doesn't even have a direct list of customers?

It's simple.

The answer is all around him.

Being downtown, he is surrounded by skyscrapers full of working people. These people have stomachs. So he could make a list of the 100 most staffed companies near him and then apply the bi-weekly contact and follow-up call attempts described above. His goal would be to reach a decision-maker he could arrange daily bulk purchasing deals with.

In fact, his costs are so low, he might not even need to offer a discount. Instead he might try emphasizing convenience as the primary value and USP. He can test it either way.

He is in another unique position. He would be better off using slow periods of the day to deliver the lumpy mail himself. Since direct in-person selling has always been more powerful than mail.

And the lumps in this case might be a couple of sample sandwiches placed on napkins on top of his message.

What would he write in the letters? Anything that would help him secure the meeting. From how convenient it would be for the employees and management. He could explain how this would help keep more of them in the office. This would help employees spread ideas around, and generate inspiration that could help the company. It's like how major companies like Pixar, Apple, and Google try to keep employees on-site to more likely generate inspiration and value for the company.

This could also complement or even replace a current arrangement with another catering provider.

He could even reference studies on the health benefits of the cheese and butter he's using, including psychologically as comfort food.

His goal should be to make a list of all benefits, really digging down like in my above examples, until he has enough ideas for a year's worth of messages.

Then as contracts come in, he can hire delivery people (ideally aligning all the offices in each building in the same delivery time range). As he secures new clients, he'll cross them off his Dream 100 and then seek out new replacements for his list to keep the number at 100. Then he'll get more trucks to cook more sandwiches and expand further and further and… well, I hope you can see the power and potential of the Dream 100 idea, even with a silly example such as this.

The idea of the Dream 100 is explored more in the great Chet Holmes book 'The Ultimate Sales Machine.'

You should try applying it to your own business and industry. Though unlike with our food truck example, you should consider improving your success with this method by harnessing the relevant services mentioned throughout this book.

Just imagine one of your Dream 100 prospects checking you out after receiving your correspondence. Remember that statistic showing 90% of prospects will check you out before considering doing business with you. So when they check you out, what would they see?

Would they see a slow website (they had to scroll through multiple pages of Google to find) and maybe no other proof of existence aside from a 3-star review from a random industry site (along with a Facebook profile that hasn't been updated in so long that Facebook deactivated it without your knowledge)?

Or, would they see an easy-to-find GMB profile and website near the top of Google along with a plethora of recent positive reviews, plus multiple active social media accounts posting relevant valuable content daily and people just like your prospect happily engaging with this content?

The answer is entirely up to you.

Now you know the powerful idea of Dream 100 and how it can help you find and secure your most profitable customers.

Next, we'll look at how to best market your business in a down economy.

Exercise:

1. Figure out who your dream customers are. Ask questions like:
   - What are the top websites they browse?
   - What businesses do they like?
   - Why do they like those businesses?
   - What type of content do they enjoy?
   - What do they find valuable?
2. Choose your Dream 100 customers.
3. Choose the gifts you mail them.
4. Create your prospecting letters (yes, letters, NOT email).
5. Create your calendar. A good example might be every two weeks over a year.
6. Make follow-up calls based on the calendar.

7. Set up a meeting to pitch each prospect.

8. As you convert Dream 100 prospects, replace your list entries with new prospects to keep the number at 100.

CHAPTER TWENTY-ONE

How To Thrive From A Poor Economy

You might be thinking this all sounds great, but there's a problem.

You're reading this book during a down economy and not sure if the same strategies will work or even if you can afford them.

So what should you do?

First of all, don't worry, I'm writing this revised book in the middle of a pandemic that is hurting many businesses more than any recession ever could. Yet some businesses are still doing fine, and others are even thriving. What gives?

Let's look at the historical best practices of what to do during an economic downturn.

A study by Ogilvy & Mather showed companies that spent more on marketing than their competition during an economic slump captured 32 to 40% more of their market, versus capturing only 15% for those who spent less. And the return on investment for those who spent more was 41%, versus 9% for those who spent less.

* * *

Fig. 32. David Ogilvy. Image credit: Wikimedia Commons by Rob Mieremet / Anefo

This isn't anything new.

This has been the pattern throughout the decades, depressions, and recessions of the past. And it will be the same throughout future down economies.

Why is that?

When an economy slows, a lot of dumb business owners cut their marketing budget. That's dumb because it's the only part of their budget that directly goes toward increasing profits. This assumes they have profitable marketing in the first place, which is something they had better prioritize fixing, especially in an economic slump.

It's also what the bottom 95% does, so by definition it's the wrong thing to do for that reason alone.

And since 95% of your competition will be doing it, that leaves them vulnerable to your aggressive marketing efforts. That's why, as Ogilvy & Mather found, the correct response is to ramp up marketing investment during a slump.

This is like how some of the most successful real estate investors wait for a market downturn to invest at rock bottom prices. That's so when the market rebounds, their investments would do best.

I like the relevant Dan Kennedy quote:

"Tigers starve last in the jungle."

On that note, I have a good example of a Realtor client of mine who took my advice. He continued advertising during the initial hard months of the 2020 pandemic. It was particularly hard for him, because not only were there later lockdowns that prevented him from showing houses (in any way except virtually). But even when there weren't lockdowns, people were too anxious to show up. So his income from selling homes plummeted and things didn't look great.

But I encouraged him to continue advertising and generating leads for one big reason. Since I knew at the very least he was building and nurturing a large list of people who were interested in buying their dream home. And I knew that as soon as things opened up and the market felt safe and comfortable, these people would start blossoming like seeds planted on a farm. And best of all, he'd be the one to close them, and not any of his competitors with their heads buried in the sand.

And that's exactly what happened.

In fact, it led to a fun video interview I did with him just short of a year since the pandemic started. I learned that in the previous month he had sold four homes... even though he was in lockdown for three of those weeks.

Now of course, he had some people helping him, but as someone who wrote a literal book on headlines, it's hard to beat that example as a way to sell the idea of investing in marketing during a slump.

Otherwise the Ogilvy & Mather study showed the value in just hunkering down and investing in the advertising vectors with highest ROI. Then one could keep building their list so that when an economic downturn is over and things start to ramp up in their region, they'd be ready to pounce and convert all these people who were waiting for a chance to hire someone like them for their services. And their competition won't believe it.

You've now learned how investing more in profitable marketing during a down economy, like every other chapter in this last section of the book, can help you further leapfrog your competition.

Next, we'll discuss a little money-management secret that could boost your income.

Exercise:

1. If you're in a down economy, audit your business expenses, and try to minimize them only in areas that don't directly (or indirectly) add to your profits.

2. Then, if possible, shift some of these savings into additional advertising investments that will pay off once the slump is over. Your competition won't know what hit them.

CHAPTER TWENTY-TWO

Apply The Babylon Secret To Make More Money

Want to know a secret? Here's a quick way to potentially boost your profits by investing in your future and in others.

You might have heard of the success book "The Richest Man In Babylon" by George S. Clayson. It was published in 1926, yet still ranks high on the Amazon Best Seller charts today. And it ranks even higher on the Amazon Most Read books too, despite being almost 100 years old.

People obviously find it valuable.

One of its most beneficial ideas concerns how to best invest your income.

First, if you have any debts, it recommends spending up to 20% of your income on paying them down.

Beyond debt, it recommends investing some of your income in two other areas.

It recommends putting 10% of your income into long-term investments. Any form of long-term investment account will do. It shouldn't be easy to access or withdraw from. You shouldn't see yourself touching it for decades.

And it recommends putting another 10% of your income into some sort of charity account you will put toward giving to those in need.

"Now Fraser, aside from guaranteeing at least 10% of my money won't be wasted, while also feeling good from giving to others, how can this actually make me more money?"

I'll get to that in a second.

But first, I need to go deeper by discussing a powerful variation of this thought up by the great copywriter, Dan Kennedy. He details it in his course "The Source Code."

Instead of forcing you to invest 20% of your income into long-term investments and charity, Dan recommends dedicating at least 1% of your income to each. So at a minimum, that would be 1% to long-term investments, and 1% to charity.

Do this every time you get money. Every time you get a paycheck or deposit, take off the allocated percentage.

It's important to do this regularly and consistently.

You can still invest more, even beyond the 20% total described by the Babylon book. But start with at least 1% each.

If you have a problem saving and find it tough to get through each month without habitually spending all your money, then I have a solution. You can't just stop spending your money, since it's habitual. So you must instead replace it with a different habit. A habit of saving.

And you accomplish and reinforce this habit by saving part of every paycheck, every divided, and every dollar that enters your bank. After a short time of doing this, the saving process will be habitual.

The power of consistently investing part of your money this way is it can help change your perspective, mindset, and approach to making money. By investing a small percentage of your income on a consistent basis, you end up making even more money than you would have otherwise made.

It gets better.

Dan generally says the higher the percentage you allocate, the more money you'll ultimately make.

And here's where it gets really interesting and counterintuitive.

Dan says he's found generally your income can increase even more by investing in charity than it does from investing in long-term investments.

As an example, he says if you're going to allocate 10% of your income for the two, then it's more profitable to allocate 8% to charity and 2% to long-term investments than it would be the other way around.

And people who follow this advice from the Babylon book and Dan notice, for seemingly no rational explanation, they end up more successful when they focus more on investing in others.

Though I might have one clue on the explanation. I found it in this excerpt from the book 'Psycho Cybernetics':

"It is a psychologic fact that our feelings about ourselves tend to correspond to our feelings about other people. When a person begins to feel more charitably about others, he invariably begins to feel more charitably toward himself. Persons who feel that people are not very important cannot have very much deep-down respect and regard for themselves...

Another reason that charity toward other people is symptomatic of the successful personality is that it means the person is dealing with reality. People are important. People cannot for long be treated like animals or machines or as pawns to secure personal ends. Treating everyone with respect is charity because it is not always, instantly, individually reciprocated. You cannot view it as transactional, instead you must see the big picture and act in this manner as a means of strengthening your own self-image, and as your contribution to society in general."

I like one other idea Dan has for implementing this strategy.

It concerns the charity percentage.

If you're not already investing in a specific charity, then an easy way to start giving is gross over-tipping. So instead of tipping 15 to 20%, tip maybe 30 to 40%.

Think about it.

A big problem many people have with charities is they think their money isn't getting to the people who actually deserve it. You might think either the management is stealing it all, or it's being wasted via incompetent spending when it could be spent better elsewhere.

At least this way you know it's going to someone who's working. They're at least taking action to better their position in life. And if they've done a good job, then all the better.

By witnessing their happiness and gratitude in person, you will feel the power of money differently. It will likely help motivate you to make as much of it as possible. To help make the world a happier and better place.

You can start doing this today. Put it into action the next time you use the services of a waiter, driver, barber, stylist, barista, bartender, food delivery driver, etc.

As long as they're doing a good job, try giving them a 30 to 40% tip. Try doing this for a few months. See what it does to your income. And then keep investing more and more from there.

Getting better future service from them is just a bonus.

Fig. 33. The means to accelerate the realization of your vision. Image credit: Pixabay

Another idea for improving your income via management is via making an emergency savings account. A good amount to aim for might be three months' worth of non-luxury spending. This is especially helpful for certain people who are just one missed paycheck away from financial collapse and ruin. The stress of such a position might not only eat away at their sanity, but also bottleneck their productivity and potential earnings.

So when you have three months' worth of funds in the bank, you can have room to breathe, and more easily focus on working on your business. Even if you encounter illness, accident, lawsuit, etc., you'll still have a solid cushion of time to deal with it.

And once you hit three months, you can invest at a slightly slower rate to maybe grow the emergency savings to six or even twelve months. Then you would know full well you could be out of commission for a year and still be fine. That would help you be more open to taking risks and going all out with building your business and life.

One last idea to keep in mind is don't forget to invest some of your earnings into yourself. You can't go wrong investing in healthy foods and physical activities you find fun.

This also applies to your own education. In addition to learning about business and your industry from your TOP5 friends and your own competitive investigating, you might consider investing up to 10% of your income into relevant books, industry journals, audio lectures, courses, and coaching. Both for self-development in your business and in life.

And if you're actively following the exercises in this book and are taking massive action to the point where you feel you have almost no time for anything. Then consider opting for audio variations of these educational tools. That way you could turn your car into "Automobile University" as sales coach Zig Ziglar liked to call it. Using time spent commuting and other multitasking opportunities to simultaneously improve your education via audio.

You've now learned some powerful money-management secrets. Next, we'll review the lessons of this book and help prepare you for massive action.

Exercise:

1. Set up two accounts (real or just using a piggy bank). Allocate at least 1% of your income each to a giving account and to a long-term investment account.

2. Use gross over-tipping of 30 to 40% as an easy, yet impactful way to begin fulfilling the giving account obligation.

3. Try to allocate more to the giving account than to the long-term investment account.

4. ???

5. Profit.

6. Also, try to set aside some savings into an emergency funds account. This could be 3 months' worth of living expenses at first, but then slowly be expanded to 6 and later 12 months' worth. This way you'll eliminate any stress of being wiped out from a single missed paycheck. You'll also be more open to taking greater risks and going all out when growing your business.

7. Consult with an accountant and financial planner before applying any of the ideas in the chapter. They'll know how to best implement them.

CHAPTER TWENTY-THREE

Conclusion

Congratulations! You've made it to the end of the book.

Usually, only around 5% of readers read books all the way. And from a study of Kindle readers, only 59% even opened the books they bought. In fact, only 10% of the people who buy a book read past the first chapter.

You're one of the top 5% of readers. That's a reason to feel proud.

Before we start the final chapter, I'd like to say something quickly.

If you're enjoying this book, and you haven't already left one, I'd appreciate it if you could leave a brief review of this book.

Reviews aren't easy to get, but they make a big difference when it comes to helping potential readers see the value they could receive. So I'd be grateful if you could spend just 60 seconds to review it through the app you're reading it on, even if it's just a sentence.

To do so, scroll to the bottom of the book, then swipe up and you will automatically be asked for a review.

If for whatever reason you can't leave a review that way: just go to the book's page on Amazon and leave a review there.

Thank you.

Now, back to the final chapter.

So now you're working away at all the end-of-chapter exercises (if not then go back and work on the rest right now). They're helping provide you with beneficial guidance such as:

- Find people nearby who're in the TOP5 percent of your business niche.
  - Show them value, perhaps buying them meals, to help get closer and become more successful like them.
- Drop any toxic and negative people from your life (outside of family).
- Spend more time with five TOP5 people than anyone else.
- Change your comfort zone to one that believes success is possible and you deserve it.
- Chart a refined list of positive goals for yourself.
- Reinforce and step closer to these goals with twice daily affirmations with visualizations.
- Make your bed every day as soon as you get up to start the day with success.
- Call prospects within 1 minute and make at least 6 additional optimally-sequenced call attempts to unreached leads.
- (If it applies to your business niche) Set up and use a CRM consistently to stay top of mind with your leads and customers.
- Focus on closing every prospect who is right for your service and can afford it.
- Understand every 'no' is getting you closer to the next 'yes'.
- Figure out your USP to more easily sell your value.
  - Make sure it isn't focused on cheapest pricing.
- Figure out how to maximize your perceived value to maximize your price by doing competitive analysis and talking with your TOP5 friends.
- Do a Notifications Audit.

- Spend your time only doing tasks that generate you maximum income.

- Ensure you have your GMB account, Facebook business page, and website optimally set up.

- Use a quality lead-generation provider to harness Facebook and Google ads.

- Use a Local SEO provider to get more cost-effective customers after 6 to 12 months.

- Use a reputation management provider to help maximize positive reviews and minimize negative ones.

- Use Social Media Management to free up your time, provide valuable content to your prospects, and show you're an active business.

- Know and improve your LTV to help utilize every single profitable source of customers to leapfrog your competition.

- Apply LTV ideas to maximizing the number of referrals you generate from a dedicated referral program.

- Create a Dream 100 list of your best potential customers and send them lumpy mail and follow-up calls every two to four weeks until you can schedule a meeting to pitch your offer and USP.

- Take advantage of any economic slumps to further leapfrog your competition by investing more in profitable marketing.

- Use the Babylon secret to invest in others, while getting bigger returns for yourself and your future.

- Take massive action with all of the above, as quickly and profitably as possible.

I've created a 1-page Exercise Reminder Chart to help make the end-of-chapter exercises easier to track and complete. It includes a summary of the exercises for each chapter. You can print it out and cross off the exercises as you complete them and grow your business. You'll find a link to it at the back of the book.

* * *

EASY SMALL BUSINESS IDEAS
PRINTABLE EXERCISE REMINDER CHART

PRINT THIS OUT AND HANG UP SOMEWHERE HIGHLY VISIBLE.
CROSS OFF THE END-OF-CHAPTER EXERCISES YOU'VE FULLY COMPLETED FROM THE BOOK.
TIP-TAKE MASSIVE ACTION AND TRY TO COMPLETE MANY EXERCISES SIMULTANEOUSLY.

1. WRITE DOWN 5 PEOPLE YOU SPEND THE MOST TIME WITH. OUTSIDE OF FAMILY. WRITE DOWN 5 NEAREST TOP5 PEOPLE YOU KNOW OF.	2. WRITE DOWN NEGATIVE PARTS OF YOUR COMFORT ZONE. WRITE DOWN NEW POSITIVE CHANGES TO YOUR COMFORT ZONE YOU WANT.	3. WRITE DOWN LIST OF THINGS YOU NEED RIGHT NOW. THINGS WANT AT SOME POINT. AND PERSONALITY QUALITIES YOU NEED TO GUARANTEE SUCCESS.	4. CREATE YOUR 30-DAY VISUALIZATION SCHEDULE SHEET.
5. PUT A STICKY-NOTE REMINDER ON BATHROOM MIRROR TITLED "MAKE MY BED."	6. CALL LEADS WITHIN 1-MINUTE. MAKE AT LEAST 6 CALL ATTEMPTS FOR EVERY UNREACHED LEAD. IDEALLY BETWEEN 8-9AM AND 4-6PM.	7. SETUP AND USE A CRM CONSISTENTLY (IF COMMON ENOUGH IN YOUR INDUSTRY).	8. ALWAYS FOCUS EVERY SECOND OF THE CALL ON GETTING QUALIFIED PROSPECTS CLOSER TO CONVERTING.
9. FIGURE OUT WHAT UNIQUE ASPECT OF YOUR BUSINESS IS BETTER THAN WHAT ALL YOUR LOCAL COMPETITION CAN OFFER.	10. COMPLETE THE TIME MANAGEMENT CIRCLE EXERCISE.	11. SIGN UP FOR A LEAD-GENERATION SERVICE TO GET A STREAM OF CUSTOMERS TODAY.	12. SIGN UP FOR AN SEO SERVICE TO GET A STREAM OF CUSTOMERS IN THE FUTURE.
13. SIGN UP FOR REPUTATION MANAGEMENT TO MAXIMIZE YOUR POSITIVE REVIEWS.	14. HIRE A SOCIAL MEDIA MANAGEMENT SERVICE TO PROVIDE VALUABLE CONTENT TO YOUR PROSPECTS AND SHOW YOU'RE AN ACTIVE BUSINESS.	15. CALCULATE YOUR LTV. USE THIS CALCULATION TO FIGURE OUT HOW MUCH YOU CAN SPEND ON EACH AD VECTOR TO GET A CUSTOMER. AND ALSO USE IT TO KNOW HOW MUCH YOU CAN SPEND TO GET A REFERRAL.	16. MAKE A DREAM 100 LIST OF YOUR BEST POTENTIAL CUSTOMERS. SEND LIST MEMBERS LUMPY MAIL AND FOLLOW-UP CALLS EVERY 2 TO 4 WEEKS.

Get more ideas at FraserDruet.com

Fig. 34. Exercise Reminder Chart.

You're on your way to being a TOP5 performer and beyond.

You aren't using a success plan made entirely out of "HOPE" like your bottom 95% competition. Hope on its own is the negative feeling of fear pretending to be optimism. You will instead adopt ACTION as your success plan. Replace all hope with the superior positive feelings of confidence and certainty. You'll get them as you experience your rapid success growth from taking massive action.

A quick note for those who might be feeling so called "Imposter Syndrome." I've given you tools to leapfrog over your competition at such a pace that it might not seem fair. Some might feel they don't even deserve such success, now that they've learned it's possible and within their reach.

If you are someone who feels this way. Don't worry. It's just a combination of your comfort zone and latent 5AVG acting up trying to hold you back. So just go back to those chapters and perform their exercises until you not only feel you deserve rapid success over your competition, but you also hang out with people who feel the same way.

So now you're on your way to making your business so successful it could be made turn-key and later franchised. Heck, you could even sell it and retire, or at least help accelerate your retirement.

The good news is the choice is yours. For now you're on your way to becoming more successful, you can choose anything you want. Hopefully, choosing from your refined list of goals.

The only thing required of you is to take massive action.

If you commit to taking massive action today, this will be one of the most exciting days of your life. NOT because of my book. It'll be one of the most exciting days of your life because of your COMMITMENT to the simple exercises I've outlined throughout this book.

If you or any of your business friends are in the list of niches I typically service, as mentioned in the introduction chapter, then seek me out if you want more customers in the ways detailed in this book. Though at the end of the day I can help almost any business get more customers.

Now head to FraserDruet.com/BookBonus to get your free exercise reminder chart.

NOTES

Resources

[Referenced in Chapter 7]

1. https://hbr.org/2011/03/the-short-life-of-online-sales-leads

2. Leads360: The ULTIMATE CONTACT STRATEGY. How to best use phone and email for contact and conversion success (PDF)

3. https://www.drift.com/blog/lead-response-report-2018/

4. LeadConnect study showing: "78% of Customers Buy From the First Responder"

5. http://www.pardot.com/buyer-journey

6. https://resources.insidesales.com/2014-lead-response-report/

7. https://www.marketo.com/definitive-guides/lead-scoring/

8. http://7dtheory.com/message-to-investors/best-times-phone-call-sales-statistics/

9. https://www.salesforlife.com/blog/how-900-companies-build-and-execute-successful-sales-development-teams

10. https://blog.hubspot.com/sales/sales-statistics

11. https://www.forbes.com/sites/kenrogue/2012/07/12/the-black-hole-that-executives-dont-know-about/#7d5a5dc538e3

12. https://www.forbes.com/sites/kenrogue/2012/07/12/the-black-hole-that-executives-dont-know-

about/#7d5a5dc538e3

13. https://blog.hubspot.com/blog/tabid/6307/bid/30901/30-thought-provoking-lead-nurturing-stats-you-can-t-ignore.aspx

14. https://thrivehive.com/how-to-follow-up-with-leads/

15. http://pages.velocify.com/rs/leads360/images/Ultimate-Contact-Strategy.pdf

16. https://blog.zoominfo.com/sales-follow-up-statistics/

17. https://business.linkedin.com/sales-solutions/blog/sales-reps/2017/03/5-sales-follow-up-techniques-that-build-trust

18. https://blog.zoominfo.com/20-shocking-social-selling-statistics/

19. https://blog.hubspot.com/sales/tips-to-get-an-unresponsive-prospect-talking-again

20. https://blog.hubspot.com/sales/why-responsiveness-matters-in-sales-tl

21. http://www.leadresponsemanagement.org/lrm_study

22. https://seopressor.com/blog/best-and-worst-times-to-send-emails/

23. https://blog.thomasnet.com/best-days-and-time-to-call-email-post-social-media

24. https://www.demandgenreport.com/industry-topics/data-management/3094-study-40-of-generated-leads-are-invalid-incomplete-or-duplicated

25. http://blog.boomerangapp.com/2017/05/the-one-thing-you-should-never-do-in-an-email-subject-

based-on-data/

26. http://blog.boomerangapp.com/2016/02/7-tips-for-getting-more-responses-to-your-emails-with-data/

27. https://www.gong.io/blog/cold-calling-tips/

28. https://www.gong.io/blog/discovery-call/

29. https://www.themarketingblender.com/statistics-boost-sales/

30. ABCofSalesinModernEra - Microsoft Download Center (PDF)

31. https://business.linkedin.com/content/dam/me/business/en-us/marketing-solutions/cx/2017/pdfs/Sophisticated-Marketers-Guide-to-LinkedIn-v03.12.pdf

32. https://blog.insidesales.com/inside-sales-tips/tips-on-texting-in-b2b-sales/

33. http://pages.velocify.com/rs/leads360/images/Text-Messaging-for-Better-Sales-Conversion.pdf?mkt_tok=3RkMMJWWfF9wsRonuKvBZKXonjHpfsX97u ouXa%2Bg38431UFwdcjKPmjr1YIHTcZ0aPyQAgobGp5I 5FENSLLYWKpst6cJWA%3D%3D

34. https://simpletexting.com/how-b2b-texting-can-enhance-your-communication-and-boost-sales/

35. https://www.salesforlife.com/blog/how-900-companies-build-and-execute-successful-sales-development-teams

36. https://www.outreach.io/blog/will-emojis-increase-reply-rates

37. https://www.intercom.com/starter-kits/real-time-sales

38. https://www.vendasta.com/blog/lead-response-

time

39. https://www.vidyard.com/video-for-sales-guide/

40. https://www.drift.com/blog/sales-video-trends/

41. https://www.campaignmonitor.com/blog/email-marketing/2019/05/how-to-use-videos-for-sales-outreach/

42. https://www.twilio.com/docs/glossary/what-sms-character-limit

43. https://www.textmagic.com/blog/why-millenials-love-texting-infographic/

44. https://skaled.com/lp/sales-follow-up-inbound-ultimate-guide

45. https://www.drift.com/blog/conversation-analysis/

46. https://www.intercom.com/blog/intercom-on-sales-book/

47. https://www.zipwhip.com/blog/5-texting-etiquette-tips-for-business/

48. https://www.twilio.com/learn/call-and-text-marketing/guide-to-us-sms-compliance

READ THIS FIRST

As a way of saying thank you for buying my book, here is a link to my 1-page printable **'Exercise Reminder Chart'** 100% FREE!

It will make the end-of-chapter exercises easier to track and complete. It includes a summary of the exercises for each chapter. You can print it out and cross off the exercises as you complete them and grow your business.

TO DOWNLOAD GO TO:

https://FraserDruet.com/BookBonus